The Young Naturalist

Andrew Mitchell

Edited by Sue Jacquemier and Martyn Bramwell

Designed by

and

Illustrated by Ian Jackson, Chris Shields (*Wilcock Riley*),
Alan Harris, Nick May, Carol Hughes (*John Martin Artists*), David Hurrell (*Middletons*),
David Nockels (*The Garden Studio*), Cynthia Pow (*Middletons*), John Sibbick, Susan Neale

Photographs by Bob Mazzer,
Gordon Dickinson, Ken Hoy, Ben Gaskell

Special consultant: David Beeson

Contents

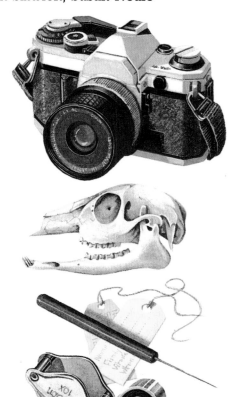

First published in 1982 by Usborne
Publishing Ltd, Usborne House,
83-85 Saffron Hill,
London EC1N 8RT, England.
Copyright © 2007, 1989, 1982
Usborne Publishing Ltd.

The name Usborne and the
device ⊕ are Trade Marks of
Usborne Publishing Ltd.

Printed in Belgium

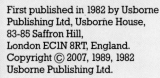

nt to be a naturalist?

There is much more to being a naturalist than simply collecting and identifying animals and plants. This book will show you how to set about detecting, observing and experimenting in the natural world around you. Each page is packed full of activities and projects you can do yourself, or with friends, and by doing them you will make many discoveries of your own. You will be able to help conservation at the same time.

The first part of the book will help you to look at individual animals and plants, while the second part shows you how to study them together – as a living community. Understanding how nature works is fascinating, and fun, and also very important because our own existence depends on it. We, too, are animals, so looking at nature helps us learn about ourselves as well. If you try most of the ideas and projects in this book you will be well on the way to becoming a naturalist.

The Zoologist studies animal life.

The Ecologist studies the relationships of animals and plants to each other and to their surroundings.

The Naturalist specializes in none of these but has an interest in each.

The Botanist studies plant life.

What a naturalist needs

All you need to start with is an enquiring mind – and your eyes, ears, nose and hands. Use all your senses to gather information from the world around you, and keep a *nature diary* (see p.24) throughout the year. Your notes will help you remember what you have seen, and they will be very useful if you join a natural history society.

A *notebook* and *pencils* are the main items of equipment but the young naturalists on the opposite page have several other very useful things with them. A *clip-board* can be made from a piece of hardboard and a bulldog clip; *yoghurt pots* and small *plastic bags* will keep small specimens safe and dry; a pair of 8×30 *binoculars* will be ideal for most observers, and a small (×10) *hand lens* or a good *magnifying glass* is a "must" for looking at tiny specimens. A good *map* will enable you to plot your discoveries and will also help you find new places to explore. It is a good idea to learn how to use a *compass* to get your bearings, and so that you can note the direction of the wind, or a flock of migrating birds, in your notebook.

Most of the equipment needed for the projects in this book can be made simply and cheaply at home. Why not build up your own mini-laboratory, with your projects and collections on display?

Towards the back of this book you will learn about the role of new technology in nature. There are *special lenses* for photographing insects, *microcomputers* to help get the most from your records, *tape recorders, bat detectors* and *radio tracking devices.*

This is the symbol of the World Conservation Strategy, a global plan put forward by the Worldwide Fund for Nature, and other conservation bodies, to stimulate wide use of the world's natural resources. Look for the symbol in the book to find out how you can help to protect nature.

Look out for the Boffin's Box symbol. It marks more difficult projects for specialists and real enthusiasts to try. You may need help with some of them.

Food for thought

This page illustrates some of the topics covered in this book. There are many more. You may wish to specialize in birds or plants, but remember that they live in competition with others. Whenever you study an animal or plant, try to work out how it is connected with the other living things around it. Naturalists learn to understand nature by having an interest in every aspect of it.

Looking at plant power. Experiments at home and projects outdoors. Flesh-eating plants and plants that move. How to make spore prints. (pp.4/5)

Flowers and insects. Who needs who in the pollination business? Pressing leaves and watching trees. Making wall charts from your observations. (pp.6/7)

Who eats who in the invertebrate underworld? The role of small animals, and how to catch them. Watching worms and making pitfall traps. (pp.8/9)

Studying life cycles and dipping into ponds. How to breed butterflies and how to set up an aquarium. Keeping ants in a formicarium. (pp.10/11)

Watching bird behaviour. How to invite birds into the garden. Understanding bird songs. Where to put nest boxes and how to build a hide. (pp. 12/13, 22/23)

Tracking down mammals: what to look for and where to find them. Mapping mole hills, finding voles, and how to look for roosting bats. (pp. 14/15)

Looking at ecosystems. Finding out how a woodland works. Making leaf litter surveys and finding animal signs. (pp. 16/17) Studying the seashore community. (pp. 18/19)

Wildlife in the city. How you can explore the urban jungle, and make a back-street nature survey. Bringing a derelict plot to life again. (pp.20/21)

Collections: how to build them up and how to use them. How to display spider webs, clean animal bones and make plaster casts of footprints. (pp. 24/25/26)

Experimenting with plants

Plants are surprisingly aggressive. They compete with each other for light, water and food. Some of the experiments on these pages will show you how they do this. But don't expect results overnight: plants take time to grow. Remember that young plants are delicate, so treat them with care.

Plants convert the sun's energy into food energy that can be used by other organisms. They are at the base of the food chain (see pp. 16/17), so we start with the plants and move on to animals later in the book.

Ways of watching germination

Most plants grow from seed or spores, and each of these experiments will tell you something more about how they do it.

1. Place soil samples from different areas in shallow dishes, then keep them warm and moist and see what germinates.

2. Bake some soil in the oven to kill any seeds in it. Place it outdoors in a tray (mid summer is the best time) and in a few days seeds will germinate. Do you know where they came from?

3. A bean, a glass jar and some blotting paper are all you need to grow a beanstalk (see below). The seed contains food for the new plant. Watch the growth of roots and rootlets, stems and leaves. You can plant it outdoors later.

Measuring plant power

Underside of potato is peeled — Sugar — Water — Water

Plants are very powerful. You have probably seen them push up through roads and pavements. The stems grow and swell by drawing water into their cells from outside. This process is called osmosis. You can see it in action by scooping out a potato, peeling a strip off the underside, and standing it in water. If you place a teaspoonful of sugar inside and leave it for a few hours, the potato will fill with water as the strong sugar solution in the cavity is diluted by osmosis.

What's the tallest tree in your area?

The giant redwoods of California reach heights of more than 100 metres. The largest trees weigh over 2000 tonnes.

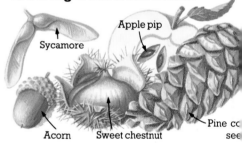

Growing trees from seeds

Sycamore — Apple pip — Acorn — Sweet chestnut — Pine cone seeds

Collect seeds from trees in autumn. Remove their tough outer coverings and place each one in a pot with soil or compost. (Soak acorns and other hard nuts in warm water overnight to make them easier to peel.) Keep the pots under cover outdoors through the winter and bring them indoors in the spring. Germination can take months.

The fight for light

Foil caps

Seedlings

Plant tips have chemicals in them that help them seek light. Grow some grass seedlings in a little soil and place foil caps on half of them when they are about 3 cm high. Place them near the window and those without the caps will bend towards the light.

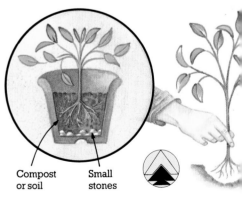
Compost or soil — Small stones

You could help increase the number of trees in your area by planting out your seedlings. Contact your local conservation group for advice on where they are needed most. It is best to plant only native species so that the local wildlife gets most benefit.

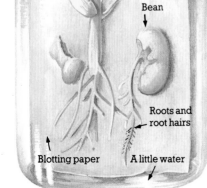
Bean

Roots and root hairs

Blotting paper — A little water

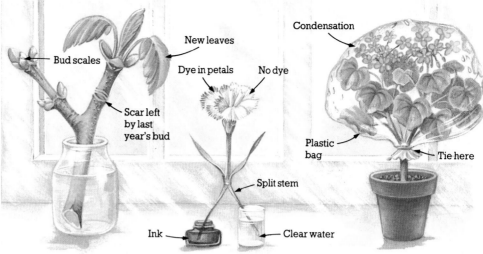

A closer look at leaves

Leaves are like solar panels that mix water and nutrients from the soil with carbon dioxide from the air and, using the sun's energy, turn them into food. The green chlorophyll pigment in them acts as the energy converter and the process is called photosynthesis.

1. Bringing buds into leaf. A winter bud contains the beginnings of next year's leaves and flowers, wrapped in protective scales. Cut some twigs from a tree (willow, birch and horse chestnut are best) and place them in clean water in a sunny spot indoors. Leaves will appear in a few weeks' time. You will see them change colour as the chlorophyll in them builds up.

2. Do leaves make rain? a) First show that plants take up water. Split the stem of a carnation and place one half in a jar of water and the other in water coloured with ink or dye. After some hours, the dye will appear in the leaves. Can you see the tiny veins through which it passes? Now show that plants lose water to the air from their leaves:

b) Tie a plastic bag around a pot plant making sure there is a tight seal round the stem. Water evaporating from the tiny pores in the leaves will condense on the inside of the bag. The process is called evapo-transpiration. Moisture carried into the atmosphere from forests from this process may end up in rain-clouds. So plants do help to make rain!

Plants on the move

Many flowers move to follow the sun's track across the sky and some have petals that close when it is dark. The leaflets of *Mimosa pudica* collapse if touched, and this makes them look less attractive to hungry animals.

Plant or animal? On an old moist tree stump you might find a jelly-like mass belonging to a slime mould. These odd fungi slither over rotten material, stopping periodically to produce their coloured spores. You can bring some home on a piece of wood for your home laboratory. Examine the mould with your lens. What can you discover about it?

This close-up shows the shiny mass of the slime mould *Lycogala epidendrum*.

Plants without leaves

Fungi have no chlorophyll and so cannot use the sun to make food. Instead they feed on other organic material – both living and dead. They spread by producing millions of tiny spores which you can see by making a spore print. Cut the stalk from a mushroom and place the cap on some paper overnight. It will release its spores in a pattern on the paper and you can preserve this by spraying it with artist's fixative. (Some fungi are poisonous, *so always wash your hands.*)

Plants that eat dead bodies!

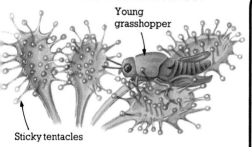

The sundew obtains nitrogen for growth by eating insects! This enables it to live where nitrogen is scarce. Try getting one from a plant shop to see how it works. Look for them growing wild in wet heathland and boggy areas. How many other types of flesh-eating plants can you find out about?

Making a bottle garden

Put some gravel, then a bed of compost, in the bottom of a large glass or plastic container such as a sweet jar, and add a few pieces of decorative bark. Collect a variety of small ferns and mosses from your street or garden and press them carefully into the soil using a pair of sticks as tools. Dampen the soil well and then pack it down firmly with a cork on the end of a stick. Put the top back on the bottle very firmly to trap in all the moisture and then watch the plants grow with no further watering.

Have a close look at the ferns with your hand lens. Try growing them by collecting spores from underneath the leaves and putting them on a fragment of clay pot in a saucer of water. Note each stage of growth as the spore develops into a new plant.

Looking at flowers and trees

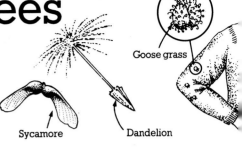

Goose grass

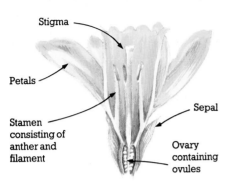

Stigma

Petals

Stamen consisting of anther and filament

Sepal

Ovary containing ovules

Flowers form part of the reproductive system of the most advanced groups of plants. They were not created to please the human eye but to attract insects (and in some cases birds). Lured by the flowers' bright colours and rich scents, these visitors act as pollinators and so help the plants to reproduce.

This picture shows the internal parts of a flower. Examine a specimen with your hand lens and try to identify the parts. Pollen from the stamens will fertilize other flowers. If it reaches an ovary, through the stigma, it fertilises the ovules to produce seeds. But how does the pollen get there?

Dispersing the seed

After pollination, flowers "set" their seed. Look for those carried by the wind; they may be spinning like helicopter rotor blades or held aloft on parachutes of fine hairs. Some seeds are covered with tiny hooks and these "hitch" rides on passing animals.

Sycamore   Dandelion

You will often find hooked seeds on your clothes after a country walk.

Experiments with bees and flowers

1. Watch a bee as it collects nectar from a flower. Can you see yellow pollen sticking to the hairs on the bee's body? Keep track of the bee as it flies off, and try to work out which flowers it visits most often.

2. Get up as soon after dawn as you can and choose a flower with lots of insect activity around it. For 15 minutes every hour note how many times the flower is visited by an insect, keeping a record of the number of different types of insect you see. Does the pattern of activity change during the course of the day? You could plot your results on a graph as shown here. Repeat this experiment with other flower species. Are the visiting insects the same or different? Try making a chart to show what kinds of visitors different flowers attract.

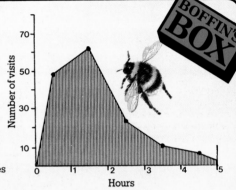

BOFFIN'S BOX

3. Do bees prefer flowers of a particular colour? You can test this by putting a blob of honey on several pieces of card, each of a different colour. See which card is most popular with the bees. Are there many flowers of this colour in your garden?

Attracting visitors

Imagine you are a bee. Which flower would you find most attractive? Different combinations of colour, shape and scent lure different insects. Look for convenient landing stages, markings that draw the eye to the centre of the flower, and a host of other navigation aids provided by the flowers for their welcome guests.

Pansy

Foxglove

Spots

Flies are attracted by scent and are trapped in the flower

Wild arum

Pollen cloud

Pine

Some flowers rely on wind or even water to spread their pollen. The flowers are often very small and hard to see. Look for them on coniferous trees in the spring.

Preserving plants and their leaves

Using the methods shown here, you can preserve leaves and also make attractive pictures with them. Leaves can be kept in their natural condition if you stand leaf-bearing twigs in a 50-50 mixture of water and glycerine for a few days. When glycerine oozes from the leaves, wipe off the excess and the leaves should retain a fresh and natural appearance for some time.

1. Place contrasting shaped leaves on sheets of plain paper and then spray them lightly with aerosol paint to leave outlines of their shapes.

2. Make a leaf rubbing by placing a dried leaf between a stiff card and a sheet of plain paper. Shade the paper over the area of the leaf with a wax crayon or pencil.

3. Small plants and flowers can be pressed between sheets of paper, weighted with heavy books or bricks. (Avoid picking wild flowers as many of them are becoming rare. Good field guides list the species protected by law.)

4. Keep your leaf prints and dried and pressed specimens in a loose-leaf book or folder as a reference collection. Each sheet should have a neat label or written notes giving the name of the species, where it was collected, the date, and any other interesting information.

NEVER PICK WILD FLOWERS OR PLANTS. THEY MAY BE RARE OR A PROTECTED SPECIES.

Looking at a tree as a community

Trees are the largest flowering plants on earth and they provide food and shelter for a multitude of living things. You can think of them as nature's apartment blocks, with a constantly-changing population of animals and plants just waiting to be discovered and enjoyed. Why not adopt a tree in your neighbourhood and follow it through the cycle of the seasons? Photograph your tree at different times of the year, make notes, take samples of its plant and animal "lodgers", and you will build up a fascinating story of the life of the tree community. The true naturalist is interested in much more than simply giving the tree its correct name. Here are just a few ideas to start you off. Use your field guides to identify creatures but always try to work out how they relate to other "residents".

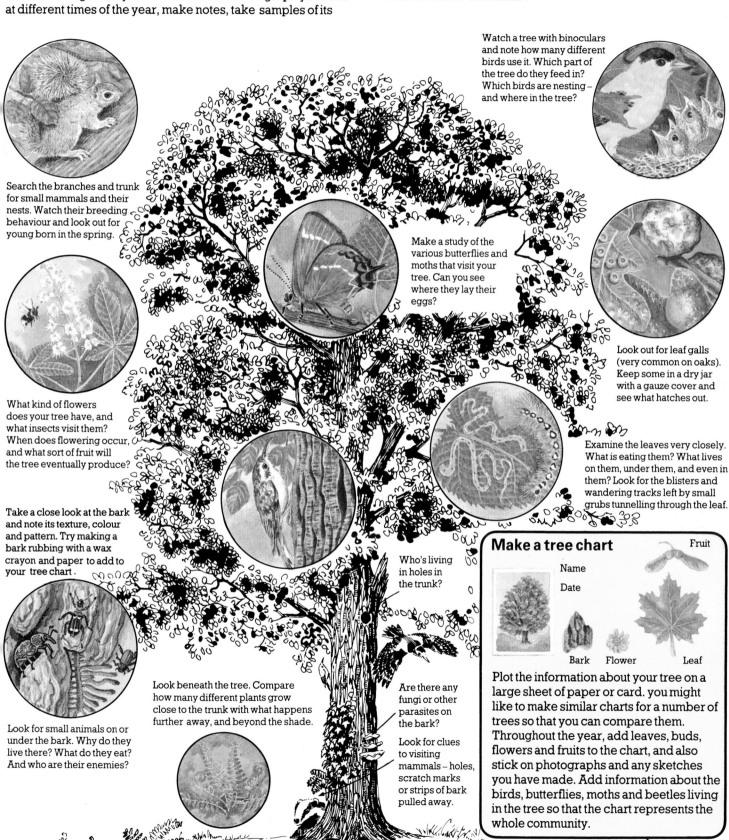

Search the branches and trunk for small mammals and their nests. Watch their breeding behaviour and look out for young born in the spring.

What kind of flowers does your tree have, and what insects visit them? When does flowering occur, and what sort of fruit will the tree eventually produce?

Take a close look at the bark and note its texture, colour and pattern. Try making a bark rubbing with a wax crayon and paper to add to your tree chart.

Look for small animals on or under the bark. Why do they live there? What do they eat? And who are their enemies?

Watch a tree with binoculars and note how many different birds use it. Which part of the tree do they feed in? Which birds are nesting – and where in the tree?

Make a study of the various butterflies and moths that visit your tree. Can you see where they lay their eggs?

Look out for leaf galls (very common on oaks). Keep some in a dry jar with a gauze cover and see what hatches out.

Examine the leaves very closely. What is eating them? What lives on them, under them, and even in them? Look for the blisters and wandering tracks left by small grubs tunnelling through the leaf.

Who's living in holes in the trunk?

Look beneath the tree. Compare how many different plants grow close to the trunk with what happens further away, and beyond the shade.

Are there any fungi or other parasites on the bark?

Look for clues to visiting mammals – holes, scratch marks or strips of bark pulled away.

Make a tree chart

Fruit

Name

Date

Bark Flower Leaf

Plot the information about your tree on a large sheet of paper or card. you might like to make similar charts for a number of trees so that you can compare them. Throughout the year, add leaves, buds, flowers and fruits to the chart, and also stick on photographs and any sketches you have made. Add information about the birds, butterflies, moths and beetles living in the tree so that the chart represents the whole community.

The role of small animals

The arthropods, a group that includes insects, spiders, centipedes, millipedes and crustaceans, account for 80 per cent of all the animals on earth. With worms, slugs and snails they belong to a huge class of animals called invertebrates (animals without backbones) and they can be found in almost every type of habitat. These pages tell you how to go about looking for them.

When investigating small animals always make a note in your nature diary of where you found them and what they may have been feeding on. Draw out food chains for each one if you can. A snail feeds on leaves but may then be eaten by a bird which in turn might be caught by a cat. Think how each animal is connected with its neighbours in this way.

Not even a specialist could identify all the animals you might find, but a good field guide will include all the most common species. Always handle tiny animals with care; it is very easy to damage them. Put them back where you found them when you have finished studying them.

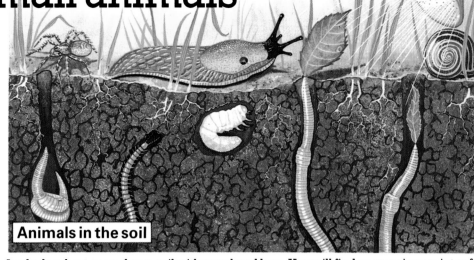

Animals in the soil

Look closely at some damp soil with your hand lens. You will find an amazing variety of creatures there. The most important animals are the earthworms: they burrow through the soil, mixing and aerating it, living off decaying plant matter. Creep into your garden at night and you may see them at work, pulling leaves down into their burrows.

Making a worm farm ▶
First of all prepare a large glass jar by filling it with damp sand and soil in alternate layers. Use a watering can to soak a patch of lawn with a dilute mixture of water and washing-up liquid. Collect the worms that come to the surface and rinse them immediately in tap water. Place the worms in the jar and add a layer of grass and dead leaves for them to feed on. Cover the jar with thick paper and leave it for a few days, then peel away the cover and look at what the worms have done. Sketch the different parts of an earthworm and see if you can work out how they reproduce.

Looking at slugs and snails

These animals live on growing plants and can be a serious pest in the garden. Look for them on and under plants at night, and on walls and tree trunks. In daytime, look in damp places where the slugs and snails hide to avoid drying out. Flower pots make a favourite hide-out. Place a slug on a sheet of glass and look from below. How does it move?

Hunting with pitfall traps

Get some jam-jars and bury them with their tops level with the surface (see below), covering them with a roof of stone or bark to keep out rain. Bait with meat, fish or cheese and try comparing the catch from a variety of habitats – for example under a hedge, or near a compost heap.

Using a pooter

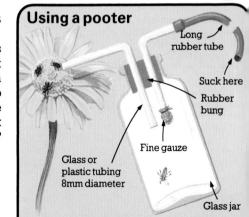

Long rubber tube

Suck here

Rubber bung

Fine gauze

Glass or plastic tubing 8mm diameter

Glass jar

How can you catch an insect without touching it? Try making a pooter! A milk bottle or jar will do for the container, which should be assembled as shown above. Pooters are ideal for "vacuuming up" small insects from flower heads or among leaf litter. Just make sure you suck at the right end! Examine your catch in a dish, sorting the creatures into groups with the aid of a fine paint brush. Once you have identified the catch, release the specimens in their own habitat as soon as possible.

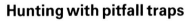

Playing tunes to spiders

If you know someone with a musician's tuning fork, try borrowing it for this experiment. Set the fork vibrating and touch the point against one of the long radiating threads of a spider's web. The spider will dash out to the attack, thinking it is a trapped fly!

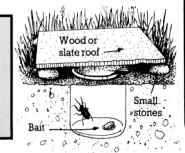

Wood or slate roof ➤

Small stones

Bait

Beating bushes and netting insects

Look at a bush carefully and see what animal life you can find on its leaves and stems. Are spiders building webs, caterpillars chewing leaves, or bugs sucking at the stems? Observation is the first step in understanding nature.

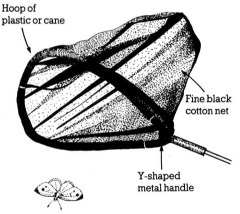

Try collecting from bushes and trees by hitting a branch sharply with a stick and catching the creatures as they are shaken loose. Use a beating tray, a piece of material stretched over a wood frame, or even an upturned umbrella. Pooter up your catch for examination.

Hoop of plastic or cane

Fine black cotton net

Y-shaped metal handle

Flying insects can be caught in a net made from a pair of tights and a wire coat hanger. A proper net can be bought, or you can make one like that shown above. The bag should be as long as your arm so that the end can be flipped over the frame to trap the insect inside. Be very gentle with butterflies: they are easily damaged. Release each specimen as soon as you have identified it.

Many butterflies are now rare due to destruction of their habitats and even to over-collecting. It is now illegal to catch some species.

Undertakers of the insect world

A dead bird or rat brought in by a dog or cat can be the start of a fascinating experiment. Peg the body under some wire mesh in the garden or under a hedge. Note each day what insect visitors appear and how they use the food supply. Maggots from blowfly eggs may be predated upon by ground or rove beetles. Burying beetles may dig soil from beneath the carcass to bury it. These animals are "decomposers", another vital link in the food chain.

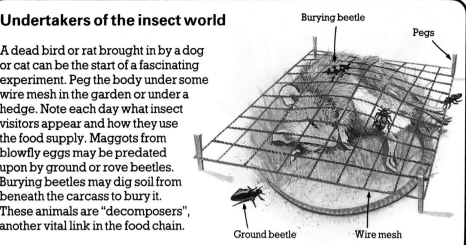

Burying beetle

Pegs

Ground beetle

Wire mesh

Sweeping meadows

Collect grassland insects with a sweep net made of white linen supported on a sturdy wooden frame e.g. an old tennis racquet. (The net needs to be strong as it takes quite a buffeting in use.) Walk steadily through long grass, sweeping the net back and forth in front of you, stopping frequently to see what you have caught. Do different grasslands contain different insects? And does insect colour show any variation with differences in grass colour?

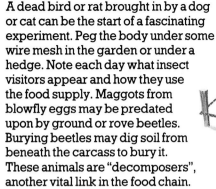

Catching the night-time fliers

Many insects prefer the hours of darkness for their activities, the best-known being the moths, though some fly by day. Here are a few ways in which night-fliers can be caught.

Sugaring. Buy some black treacle and add a few drops of amyl acetate ("pear drops" – you can get it from a chemist) and also a spoonful of beer. Paint the mixture onto posts or tree trunks on a warm still night and watch what flies in for a taste.

▲ An electric light bulb on a long lead from your house can also work well, and results are further improved if you use a mercury vapour (MV) lamp. Their ultraviolet light is extremely attractive to night-flying insects.

Light traps. There are many types but the simplest is a powerful gas or incandescent kerosene lamp placed on a white sheet laid on the ground. The lamp is best raised on a box. This works well in woodland but in open places try hanging the sheet on a gate or hedge with the lamp in front of it. Use a pooter for small specimens, a jar for large ones.

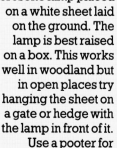

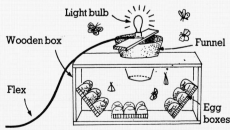

Light bulb

Wooden box

Funnel

Flex

Egg boxes

A simple light-box trap like this can be made very cheaply, and you can leave the light on all night – examining your catch the following morning.

Looking at life cycles

Here are just a few examples of life-cycles you might like to study. Look around the natural world and you will find many more worth investigating.

A dung beetle observatory

Like us, nature tries to avoid wasting energy, and surprisingly there is plenty of energy in dung. You can burn it, or use it as fertilizer, but dung beetles eat it. They collect dung from cowpats or sheep and rabbit droppings and drag it into underground tunnels for their larvae to feed on. You can watch them do this, but first you need a beetle den.

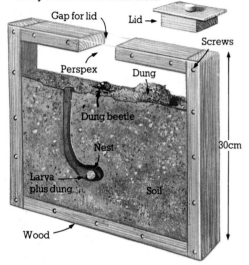

Gap for lid
Lid →
Screws
Perspex
Dung
Dung beetle
Nest
Larva plus dung
Soil
Wood
30cm

What you need: Four lengths of wood, 30cm long by 3cm wide, 2 perspex or glass panels, 30cm square, and some screws. Assemble as shown above, drilling the perspex to take screws or gluing the glass in place to form a thin box. Add fine soil and some leaf litter to within about 10cm of the top. Make a small lid. Collect some beetles from fresh dung, put them in the observatory, add several lumps of dung – and watch. The beetles bury the dung and lay their eggs: later the larvae will burrow to the surface.

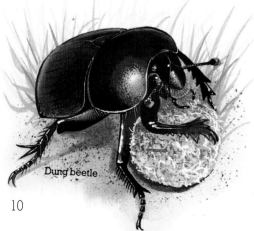

Dung beetle

Rearing butterflies

Red Admiral butterflies are found all over the world. The pattern on the underside of their wings was once thought to resemble the Devil's face. You can rear them – and many other species – from caterpillars collected in the wild. Just follow these steps:

1. Buy a rearing cage like the one on the right from a dealer if you can: they give the best results. Alternatively, make one from a cardboard box with gauze covering the open front (see below). Cut out one end so that the box can stand over a pot containing the caterpillar's preferred food plant (it will be the plant you found it on).

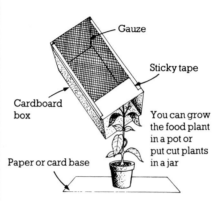

Gauze
Sticky tape
Cardboard box
You can grow the food plant in a pot or put cut plants in a jar
Paper or card base

2. In the spring and summer, search for caterpillars on trees, bushes and weeds – always bringing home some of the plant on which you find them. (A field guide will help identify unfamiliar plants.) You will find Red Admiral caterpillars wrapped up in nettle leaves. To keep food-plants fresh, stand them in a jam-jar with water – but keep nettles and thistles in a dry jar as they tend to go soggy in water.

Painted Lady

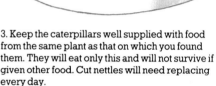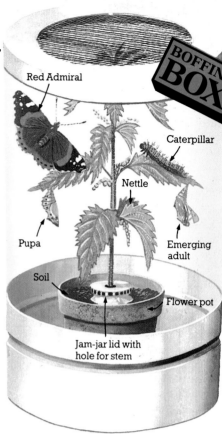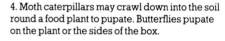

BOFFIN'S BOX

Red Admiral
Caterpillar
Nettle
Pupa
Emerging adult
Soil
Flower pot
Jam-jar lid with hole for stem

3. Keep the caterpillars well supplied with food from the same plant as that on which you found them. They will eat only this and will not survive if given other food. Cut nettles will need replacing every day.

4. Moth caterpillars may crawl down into the soil round a food plant to pupate. Butterflies pupate on the plant or the sides of the box.

5. Wait for the adults to emerge. This will vary according to species and the temperature. Most species take ten days or more.

6. Release the adults soon after they emerge as they will need to feed. If you have the right plants the butterflies may remain in your garden (see also pp. 22/23).

◄The Painted Lady is another very attractive species you might try. Look for black caterpillars underneath thistle leaves.

Contact your local conservation group and see if you can help by breeding endangered species to release in your area. Eggs can be bought from dealers. There are good books on butterfly breeding (p. 32).

Keeping an ant colony

You can also use a beetle den for studying ants. Best of all are the black garden ants which nest beneath stones on wasteland. Collect them with a pooter, or brush them into a jar from a lifted stone. Make sure you include a queen (she is larger than the workers). Put the ants in the den along with a wad of wet cotton wool and a bottle-top full of honey, and see them build tunnels and nest chambers.

Dipping into ponds and rivers

The edges of ponds and rivers are great places for naturalists to explore – but be careful not to fall in! It is safer if there are two of you. Peg a length of string from the bank top to the water's edge and examine the plant-life along the line. How do plants change in form from dry land to water? Does the animal life also change along the line?

Using your net, try sweeping the water surface, the mid-levels and the bottom. Compare your catches. Lift out some stones and mud (replacing them after you've finished) and see what lives there. Look on plant stems too. How are the animals adapted to their own particular living conditions?

Always take plenty of jars or plastic containers for your samples. You need a net (or a household sieve will do) and a hand lens, as well as your notebook. Pick up tiny specimens with an eye-dropper.

Making a natural aquarium

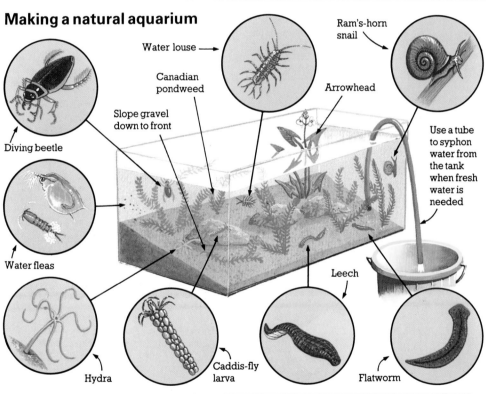

Water louse

Canadian pondweed

Ram's-horn snail

Arrowhead

Slope gravel down to front

Diving beetle

Water fleas

Use a tube to syphon water from the tank when fresh water is needed

Hydra

Caddis-fly larva

Leech

Flatworm

Why not keep a "natural" pond in your home? A large glass jar will do, but a large tank is better. First get some gravel and wash it thoroughly. Place it in the tank as shown here and add some river stones.

Animals need oxygen, so add plants that produce it. Arrowhead or Canadian pond weed are best. you can find them in the wild or buy them. Put some pond mud over the gravel (for the plant roots) and add pond water very gently. Pour it into a saucer to avoid disturbing the mud and gravel. Leave the tank to settle.

Now for the animals. Algae will colour the tank sides green so add some snails to eat them clean. Roundworms and flatworms may have already appeared but add some more, plus a leech or two. Collect some freshwater lice and shrimps to scavenge the bottom, and some water fleas as food for hydras. See how many life-cycles you can study in the tank.

Keeping the tank clean

If your mini-ecosystem is out of balance the water may go cloudy due to excessive growth of algae. If this occurs, syphon off the water and replace it with fresh. Alternatively, let a freshwater mussel do the job for you. Look for them half buried in river sand or mud. Add one to the tank and its filter-feeding will clear the water of algae.

Things to try

1. Watch a snail feeding on the side of the tank. Can you see its rasping tongue (called a radula) scraping off the algae? See also how it moves on its muscular foot.

2. Look out for leeches attacking thin red tubifex worms and eating them like spaghetti!

3. Hatch some mosquito larvae into adults. Have a good look at the larvae with a hand lens. Can you see how they breathe at the water surface? How do they feed?

4. Rear baby snails in a jam-jar from the jelly-like blobs of eggs you might find sticking to plants.

Snail eggs

ALWAYS RETURN LIVING CREATURES TO THEIR NATURAL HABITAT AFTER YOU HAVE OBSERVED THEM.

11

Watching birds

Birds are numerous and all around us, in town and country alike, and they are among the easiest and most rewarding creatures to watch. You can be a "twitcher", content simply to identify and list all the birds you have seen, or you can be a naturalist and try to discover just how the different species fit into the jigsaw of animal and plant life. Here are some ideas for the beginner, but remember the golden rule: the birds come first. Never harm or disturb them.

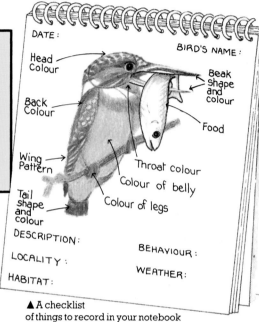

To avoid tired arms (and a shaky view) try resting your binoculars on a tripod or a rest of sticks.

How to begin

To start you need nothing more than keen eyes and patience. Get to know the birds in your garden or street first. Then try the local park, a lake or river bank and finally open country. Remember, the birds will be watching you, so be quiet and stealthy, wear dull clothing, and try to blend with the scenery. The best time to look for birds is soon after dawn or just before dusk. To get a closer view, binoculars are a "must". There are many sizes; 8×30s are lightweight and powerful enough for most purposes.

You will be surprised just how quickly you can become familiar with the common birds. How many can you name already? For the others you will need a good field guide (p. 32). Record each bird you see in

Field sketches. To help identify a bird later, note the main plumage details on a simple bird outline built up of ovals as shown here.

a notebook as shown on the right. Note its colour size, shape, and any special features or behaviour. Note where you saw the bird, and what it was doing at the time. A pocket tape recorder is useful for taking field notes as it allows you to record without losing sight of the bird.

DATE :
BIRD'S NAME :
Head Colour
Back Colour
Wing Pattern
Tail shape and colour
Beak Shape and colour
Food
Throat colour
Colour of belly
Colour of legs
DESCRIPTION :
BEHAVIOUR :
LOCALITY :
WEATHER :
HABITAT :

▲ A checklist of things to record in your notebook

What do birds do all day?

Here are some of the things a birdwatcher looks out for – the nest, the time of day the bird is active, the shape of its wings and the way it flies, and the way it acts when it is with other birds – both of its own kind and with other species. Looking at bird behaviour and discovering more about the way they live will give hours of enjoyment.

Patterns of activity. Does the early bird catch the worm? Which birds are early risers – and do you know why? When do they stop to rest, and where do they roost? Try making a timetable for an owl or a starling.

Barn owl

Starling

Courtship and aggression. Watch a male pigeon strutting and bowing in front of his chosen mate. How does she react? Look out for other courtship rituals, especially in spring, and note how birds fight over territory at this time of year. Watch for battles over food, especially when it's scarce due to hard weather. Who wins the squabbles at your birdtable?

Swallow

Pigeon

Grebe

Nesting. In spring, look for birds carrying twigs and grasses. They will be preparing their nests. See if you can follow the bird to its nest site, but don't go too close. Leave at once if the bird becomes agitated. Keep a note of when the first young appear. Look for swallows and martins under the eaves.

Movement. What style of flight does your bird have? What shape are its wings? Gliders like gulls have long narrow wings while woodland birds have short broad wings for powerful flight and agile manoeuvring. How does your bird take off?

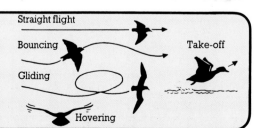

Straight flight
Bouncing
Gliding
Take-off
Hovering

Care of the young. Watch for birds carrying worms or insects; they will be feeding their brood. Listen for young birds cheeping for food from the nest and, if possible, watch the parent feeding them. Look for the many ways in which adult birds protect their young.

Do all birds eat the same thing?

Obviously not. If they did, there would be far too much competition for too little food. The different types of bill give a very good clue to the kinds of food different birds eat. Even common garden birds have preferences. Fix five or six shallow dishes to a plank, and put different food in each (worms, fat, seeds, cheese, as shown on the right). Keep a note of who eats what. Experiment with other foods. This is called a food preference study.

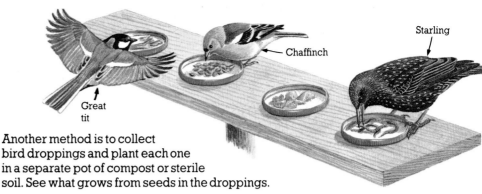

Great tit

Chaffinch

Starling

Another method is to collect bird droppings and plant each one in a separate pot of compost or sterile soil. See what grows from seeds in the droppings.

A bird for each habitat

All birds need food and living space but they avoid competition by occupying different habitats, or different parts of the same habitat. Many are specially adapted for a particular way of life. Compare the kinds of bird you find beside a river with those in a forest. Look at their feet, and bills. How are these adapted to the way they feed?

Migrating geese

Watching for migrants

Have you noticed that as the weather gets colder, some birds disappear while new ones arrive? Swallows are a good example. They, like many other species, migrate each year – spending the northern winter months in warmer countries far to the south. Keep a careful record of changes in your local bird population, especially in spring and autumn. Visit coastal reserves or inland lakes to see migrant waders.

Getting close: using hides

Careful stalking will often get you quite close to birds, but using a hide will bring more success – particularly in the breeding season when the birds are much more nervous. A car is actually a very good hide if it is driven up slowly and if the occupants keep quiet and still inside. For use in the field, a hide like the one illustrated is simple to make and exciting to use. Make the walls of canvas, painted or dyed with blotches of green and brown. Fix the frame securely and use stones to stop the walls flapping. Put the hide in place a day or two before you want to use it so that the birds get used to it. Vertical slits in the walls make the best viewing holes.

Tie the sticks together firmly with strong string or with wire.

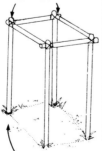

Make sure the sticks are pressed firmly into the ground.

Stop the sides from flapping by placing heavy stones around the bottom edge.

BOFFIN'S BOX

Understanding birdsong

You can always hear far more birds than you can see so it makes good sense to learn how to recognize a bird by its song alone. The best way is to go out with an experienced birdwatcher and ask him to point out the different songs and calls as you hear them. You can also borrow recordings, and videos, from many libraries and birdwatching societies. Try to learn the common species first and progress from these onto the rarer and more difficult ones. It is very good practice, and also great fun, to go out into a wood or other habitat armed with a portable tape recorder and make your own recordings of birdsong (p. 27).

Now try to work out what the different songs and calls mean. 1. Start by listening to a chicken. Try to imitate the different sounds it makes and learn what activities these are associated with. Do this with other common species. 2. What sounds do different birds make when they see a cat? 3. Many birds adopt a number of perches which they use as songposts. Make a map of the songposts of a starling, a thrush and a robin. 4. Do different birds sing at different times of day? Take one day each month and record the number of hours each known species sings. If you also record the temperature, wind, cloud cover and air pressure, you will be able to work out, for your notes, how weather conditions affect the birds' performance.

Contact your local ornithological society to see if you can help in census work or other projects.

Tracking down mammals

Mammals occur throughout the food chain, from grazers and browsers like rabbits and deer right up to the top predators like foxes, pine martens and wild cats. They are skilful at avoiding detection, and many of them are nocturnal and difficult to find; but don't despair – they are all around you, and with patience you might find one right under your feet. On previous pages we have worked our way up the food chain from the lower plants and the invertebrates up to the birds and now the mammals, gradually discovering more about how the food chain works. The illustration on the right shows a very simple chain (foxes eat rabbits, which eat grass); a longer one is shown on page 16. When looking at an animal, always try to work out where it fits in one of these chains. Is it hunter or hunted? And how is it equipped to survive in its natural surroundings?

Look out for invaders!

Imported foreign animals can unbalance food chains. Rabbits introduced into Australia devastated the countryside; deer in New Zealand ravage the woodlands – because in both cases there were no top predators to control them. Can you discover any mammals that have been brought into your area or ones that have escaped from captivity?

Did you know that wallabies from Australia live wild in some parts of Britain?

Mapping out rabbit warrens and mole territories

Next time you go for a walk, step softly around the edge of a field, keeping a sharp look-out. If you keep down-wind of the rabbits, you may see them before they see, or smell, you. Warm evenings after rain are always good times to try. Find a good hiding place and note the rabbits' feeding, courtship and territorial behaviour.

When you find a rabbit hole, place some twigs across the entrance and come back the next day. If the twigs have been moved, you will know the burrow is being used. Make a map of the warren, marking

Easy ones to start with

The easiest of all is man himself. Don't forget that we are mammals too and have our place in nature. Our cats, dogs and farm animals were once wild animals, so study them too.

Creeping up on cats. Practise your stalking skills by seeing how close you can get without being spotted. Domestic and stray cats have definite territories, and scientists spend a lot of time studying them. You can make your own studies.

Get to know the cats in your area. Note their favourite routes and where they hunt. Try following a tom on his daily patrol, and map his territory. Record the places he marks with his scent, and where he fights with other toms. Do any other cats use the same routes? Note how they use natural cover to hide their approach, and how they approach from down-wind.

On safari in the park. You may be lucky and see deer in the early morning in a woodland clearing, but the easiest place to see large mammals is in a park. Here they will have become used to humans and are not so timid. Next time you visit a park with animals in it, take time to watch one species for an hour or so. It could be a deer, a squirrel or even a mouse. Ask yourself these questions:
1. How is the animal camouflaged?
2. How is its body shape suited to its habitat and way of life?
3. What is it feeding on, and how?
4. How does it communicate with other animals around it?

If you live near a park, you could make observations of one species right through the year.

which holes are in use. Watch particularly for nursery burrows where the doe keeps her young.

While on your walks you will almost certainly see mole hills. The mole uses a network of tunnels between the hills, constantly hunting the worms that fall into these underground cavities. Clear away the soil from a mole hill and you will see the tunnel beneath. Map where the hills are, and come back each week to see how the mole has extended his territory. If you see a very large mole hill, don't disturb it – the mole may have its nest beneath it.

N. American star-nosed mole →

Plot a map of mole and rabbit territories.

Making your own small mammal survey

1. Describe the habitat. You might start with your garden. Draw a plan, to scale, and mark on the flower beds, lawns, bushes, earth banks and so on. If you choose an area of farmland, mark the fields and hedgerows, pastures and woodland. Use colours for the different habitats.

2. Keeping records. Each time you see a mouse or a squirrel, mark the sighting on your map and enter it up in your field notebook.

3. Tracks and signs. To become an expert you will need the help of a good field guide, but here are a few clues:
a) Search woodland margins, hedges, muddy paths and puddles for animal tracks. Look at the pattern of the track as well as the individual prints. Try making a plaster casts of good prints (see p. 26).

Roe deer — Fox — Domestic dog — Rat — Grey squirrel

▲ Harvest mice make nests of woven grass

▲ Pine cone chewed by squirrel; hazel nut opened by vole or mouse

b) Look for flattened grass, holes through hedges, narrow paths and tunnels through long grass. These are regularly used "runs" so mark them on your area map, identifying the animal wherever possible.
c) Look for nuts and fir cones that have been gnawed or split, and for pieces of bark torn from trees. Note any piles of feathers or bits of fur showing where a predator has made a kill.
d) Herbivores usually leave rounded fibrous droppings. Flesh-eaters leave elongated pointed droppings. Small white-tipped droppings are from birds or lizards.

4. Evidence from remains. Search hedges and roadside verges for bodies. You can identify them from the skulls using a good field guide. Wear gloves to pick up the specimen and, as soon as possible, place it in strong bleach for a day to disinfect it. Examine any bottles you find in a hedge. Small animals often climb inside and become trapped. Bleach the contents overnight and then rinse the bones. Look at pages 24/25 to see how owl pellets can help your local survey.

▲ Deer droppings are easy to recognize

▲ Badger hairs caught on barbed wire

▼ Look for skeletons in discarded bottles near lay-by or picnic areas.

Building a garden observation cage

This observation cage functions like a bird-table but is designed instead to attract small mammals. The cage can be built almost anywhere in the garden but the best place is right against the house, as shown here, with rat- and cat-proof tunnel entrances and, if necessary, longer enclosed runways leading away to the safety of hedges or herbaceous borders.

If possible build the frame around a ground floor window facing out onto a grassy bank or area of bushes. This allows you to watch the animals come and go without disturbing them. Cover the frame with wire mesh, not more than one-centimetre square, to keep out cats and other predators. The entrances should be small tunnels passing under the edge of the frame and should be too small for rats.

Place food such as rolled oats, peanut butter, fruit or cheese, on a platform inside the cage. Build ramps leading to it and place food on these as well as around the entrances. In time, mice and voles will become regular visitors, day and night. The key to success is *regular* feeding. The animals will only come when they have learned that the cage offers a constant source of food and a safe place in which to eat it. Hang a low-wattage red light bulb outside the window on an extension lead and you can watch the animals at night. They seem unaware of red light.

Attach the frame to the outside wall so that it cannot work loose. You can watch from indoors and even take photographs.

Use small mesh chicken wire to keep out rats.

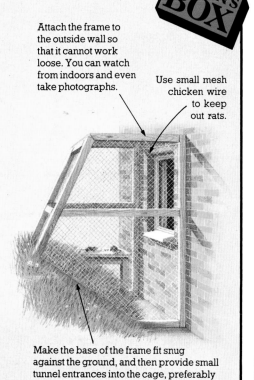

Make the base of the frame fit snug against the ground, and then provide small tunnel entrances into the cage, preferably hidden among vegetation.

Catching small animals

This can be a fascinating part of a biologist's work but specialized knowledge and equipment is needed to avoid causing suffering or accidental deaths. If you want to learn more, join a local natural history society and see how they carry out their small mammal surveys.

Do you live with bats?

On warm summer evenings, keep a look-out for bats flying around the neighbourhood. They may have come from your house! You can check in the apex of the roof and also watch for bats emerging from under the eaves. Keep watch near rivers and any other open water at dusk and note when the bats appear. Throw a small pebble into the path of a hunting bat – it may swoop after it, mistaking it for a flying insect!

Bats need friends. If you are lucky enough to discover a bat roost, do nothing to disturb it. Bats are now protected by law in many countries. You can help these fascinating creatures by building a bat box (p. 23). See p. 30 for bat detectors.

The pipistrelle is one of the most widespread and common of the European bats.

Looking at ecosystems

Up to now, you – the naturalist – have been first a botanist and then a zoologist. Now it is time to try your hand at being an ecologist too. The next few pages will show you how to explore different communities as gigantic jigsaw puzzles made up of interconnected animals and plants. Using the methods described in this book you will be able to study any community you find interesting.

Remember that every animal and plant has its own place in nature, but each is affected by the others and by the environment in which they all live. These communities of living things are called ecosystems and the study of how they work is ecology. Looking at ecosystems will give you a new view of the world about you.

Unravelling connections

Imagine you are a carbon atom floating in the air. This diagram shows how you might be recycled within a forest. Can you work out how a similar cycle might work in the ocean?

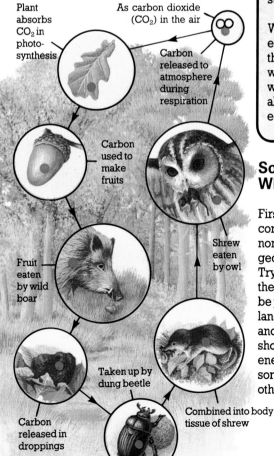

Plant absorbs CO_2 in photosynthesis

As carbon dioxide (CO_2) in the air

Carbon released to atmosphere during respiration

Carbon used to make fruits

Fruit eaten by wild boar

Shrew eaten by owl

Taken up by dung beetle

Combined into body tissue of shrew

Carbon released in droppings

Energy pathways

Just like a car engine, an ecosystem needs a power source in order to keep going. In nature this is provided by the sun. Only the green plants can convert the sun's energy into food energy, through photosynthesis. To an ecologist, the green plants are *producers,* and herbivores which live on them are *consumers.* Carnivores eat herbivores and so are called *secondary consumers,* or *tertiary consumers* if they eat other carnivores. Omnivores like badgers (and man) eat all categories.

At each stage of the food chain, from producer to consumer, less of the original energy trapped in the leaf is passed on. Some is lost as heat and waste products, so usually only three to four stages can be supported. Can you find examples of longer food chains? Here is one, illustrated right, with six links: a producer, a primary (that is, plant-eating) consumer, and a string of higher consumers.

When plants and animals die, their remaining energy and nutrients are returned to the soil or the atmosphere by *decomposers.* Nothing is wasted: it is all recycled. When looking at a woodland, or a rubbish tip, a fungus or a bird, always ask yourself how it fits into the energy equation: where on the pathway does it lie?

TERTIARY AND SECONDARY CONSUMERS

PRIMARY CONSUMER

PRODUCERS

ENERGY FROM THE SUN

RAW MATERIALS

Bird of prey

Snake

Shrew

Beetle

Caterpillar

So much for theory! Where do I begin?

First discover what plants your ecosystem contains, then list its animals. Study the non-living parts of the system such as the geology, scenery, soil type and climate. Try drawing up a chart to show how all these factors are interrelated. There will be physical cycles like the shaping of the landscape by weathering and erosion, and living cycles like the carbon cycle shown on the left. Look especially for the energy chains and try to work out why some creatures are very common while others are becoming rare.

Wondering about woodlice

Have you ever wondered how many woodlice (sow bugs) there might be in a wood? Ecologists do; and this is one of their ways of finding out.

Choose a place where there are plenty of woodlice (your garden may do if you can't get to a wood). Take an area of, say, 40 square metres and within this mark out a one-metre square using pegs and string. Then catch all the woodlice in the square, put them in a box, and count them. Mark each one with a tiny blob of model paint and then release them again inside the string boundary.

Next night, capture all the woodlice you find inside the string. Make a note of the total catch *and* the number of marked woodlice.

A first look at woodland ecology

Getting to know your wood

1. Firstly, what kind of wood have you got?
Slender spiky leaves belong to coniferous trees: wide flat leaves are typical of the broadleaved woodland trees. The latter usually lose their leaves in autumn. Few areas of natural woodland now exist in Europe: most European woods are plantations.

Maple (broadleaved)

Larch (coniferous)

2. What plants and animals are there in the wood? The more often you go there, the more you will discover about it. Use field guides to help identify flowers and mosses, insects and birds. Sit quietly in a secluded spot for an hour or two and make notes on what you see. Does the activity vary throughout the day?

3. Dig up a sample of soil and mix it with plenty of water in a milk bottle. Let it settle and note how it has separated into a number of layers. This is what happens in a lake or sea: geologists call it sedimentation. It is part of the non-living environment that affects ecosystems.

Plant matter

Water with clay in suspension

Clay

Sand

Grit and stones

Work out the population like this:

$$\frac{\text{Total number caught and marked: night 1} \times \text{Total number caught: night 2}}{\text{Number of marked insects: night 2}}$$

Multiply this "single-square" population by 40 and you will have an estimate of the total woodlouse population of your chosen area. If you work out the population for several different sample squares, the average of those results will give you a more accurate figure.

Ecologists call this the "mark and recapture" method of estimating animal populations, and it is used all over the world for creatures both large and small.

BOFFIN'S BOX

Who lives where and on what?

Once you are familiar with your wood, start looking at where different plants grow. Trees dominate the woodland jig-saw, blotting out light on which other plants depend. Remember, trees are home to complex communities (see p. 7).

How do plants respond to lack▶ of light? Measure the width and length of leaves (e.g. nettle or bramble) growing in shade and in sunlit parts of the wood. Has the difference in amount of light affected their growth? Can you show this on a graph?

▼Feeding signs. The clues shown on pp. 14/15 will help you discover what mammals are in your wood. Here are a few more. There are several good guides to tracks and field signs.

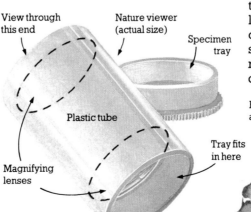

Spruce gnawed by bank vole

Bark stripped away by deer

Bark damaged by squirrels

Conifer buds gnawed by bank voles

Rushes nibbled by water voles

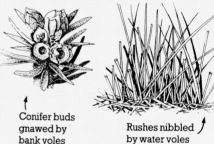

▲A wood for all seasons. If you have a camera, photograph the same patch of woodland at different times of the year. Use your pictures to help record what comes up beneath the trees before they come into leaf.

▼What animals are feeding on leaves? Examine leaves for signs of damage by browsing animals and by insects. Use a beating tray (see p. 9) to collect possible insect culprits.

A close look at the woodland floor

Nature has a team of garbage disposal workers to reclaim and recycle the useful fibre and nutrients in fallen leaves. To find them you will need to make a sieve like this with a mesh-size of about 8mm. Fill the sieve with leaf litter and then shake it gently over a dish or box while poking the leaves about with a twig. A pooter is useful for picking up small specimens (see p. 8) and a nature viewer (below) is ideal for examining them.

View through this end

Nature viewer (actual size)

Specimen tray

Plastic tube

Magnifying lenses

Tray fits in here

Many of the herbivores decomposing the leaves will be insects, but even smaller organisms are at work. Can you find the threadlike filaments of fungi on decaying leaves? These are absorbing the very last of the nutrient energy, leaving only a skeleton. The decomposers eventually return the nutrients to the soil where they can be used again by other plants.

Fungi spreading along leaf veins

17

Where the ocean meets the land

The seashore is an exciting place to explore because its astonishing range of animal life is easy to find. Like a wood, the shoreline ecosystem runs on sun power, fixed in this case by algae called seaweed and the minute floating plants called *phytoplankton*. Snail-like herbivores graze over the rocks, predators hunt their prey, and countless filter-feeders sift their food from the living "soup" of the sea.

The seashore is another living jigsaw for you to solve. Use the ideas here and on page 16 to see how it works.

Know your beach

Beachcombing is a rewarding pastime. The best place to look is along the strand line (the high point of the tide) especially after a storm. Here a multitude of seaweeds, shells, dead creatures and flotsam will be found. Look out for scavenging birds as this is their feeding ground.

Look closely at timbers for gribble and shipworm holes, and among seaweeds for sandhoppers – the woodlice of the seashore. Even plastic and metal containers disfigured with tar provide homes for small animals, especially the common goose barnacle. Make a survey of creatures living on polluted materials. You may be surprised at what you find.

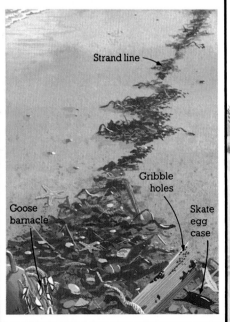

Strand line

Goose barnacle

Gribble holes

Skate egg case

What sort of shore have you got?

Is it rocky, sandy or muddy; covered in shingle, or a combination of several types? Sandy beaches are good for worms and all kinds of burrowing bivalves, but rocky shores are the richest in life. Buy a map, or make your own, and plot the areas of sand, shingle and rock. Later you can add the results of your surveys.

Clues to life beneath the sand

Hungry seabirds would make short work of any small creatures trying to live on the surface of a sandy or muddy shore. Here, life exists *beneath* the surface where filter-feeding worms and shellfish wait for the incoming tide to carry their food supply within reach. Search for siphon holes in the sand. Dig down quickly and you might discover who made them. Drop salt onto a razor-shell hole and then grab the shell as it comes up. Put it back on the sand and watch how it burrows back beneath the surface. Most of these creatures leave their signs on the surface, and they provide food for the next link in the chain – the seabirds.

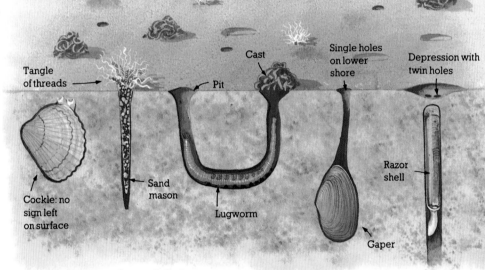

Tangle of threads

Cast

Pit

Single holes on lower shore

Depression with twin holes

Cockle: no sign left on surface

Sand mason

Lugworm

Razor shell

Gaper

Watching seashore birds

Use the techniques described on pp. 12/13 to help you get close. The best time to look for seabirds is in the early morning or evening – and as the falling tide is leaving sand and mud flats uncovered. Take a good field guide with you and see how many species you can identify.

Do the birds keep to particular zones on the beach? Look for terns diving into the water, sanderlings running beside the water's edge, oystercatchers probing the sand, and gulls scavenging along the strand line. Try to find out what birds (and mammals) live among sand dunes.

Check sand dunes for tracks and trails in the early morning

Shelduck

Who is living in the sand dunes?

Ringed plover

Gulls scavenge everywhere

Turnstones search the strand line for sandhoppers

Can limpets find their way home?

When the tide is up, limpets move over the surface of the rocks scraping off algae with their rough tongues. You can see their trails, which always return to the same spot – marked by a roughly circular groove cut into the rock by the edge of the shell.

Find a rock with a large number of limpets living on it. Look carefully at their shells and try to find several with distinctive patterns or markings. Draw an accurate plan of the limpets and the rock. Return to the rock on several occasions. Look to see the position of your limpets. Compare them with your original drawing.

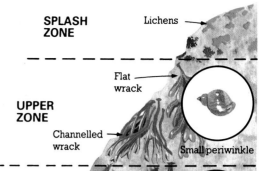

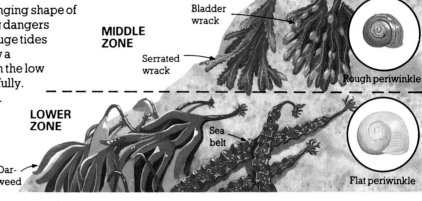

SPLASH ZONE — Lichens

UPPER ZONE — Flat wrack, Channelled wrack — Small periwinkle

MIDDLE ZONE — Bladder wrack, Serrated wrack — Rough periwinkle

LOWER ZONE — Oar-weed, Sea belt — Flat periwinkle

Drawing beach zones

The sea dominates the shoreline, carving the ever-changing shape of the beach and subjecting its residents to the alternating dangers of drowning or drying out. Whether the area is one of huge tides or small tides, the plants and animals of the shore follow a pattern which you can discover simply by walking from the low water mark to the highest tide mark – and looking carefully. Use a field guide to help you identify the things you find. On the lower shore there will be dark brown kelp and oar-weed. The middle zone is characterized by yellow brown seaweeds such as bladder wrack and serrated wrack. Green seaweeds occupy the upper zone and lichens the splash zone where only the spray reaches. Animal life also follows the zones.

Delving into rock pools

Look at a rock pool as an example of an ecosystem in miniature. What are its non-living components? Think of rock type, surface, water salinity and so on. Next list the primary producers:

phytoplankton (a bit small to see without a microscope), seaweeds and other algae. Draw their positions on a plan of the pool. Can you see zoning here too? How about herbivores? Poke about to find limpets and winkles grazing upon the rock algae. Further up

the food chain look for carniverous dog whelks and anemones, filter-feeding mussels, barnacles and corals; or even a beautiful sea slug. Tempt the larger rock pool residents into view with a bit of fish. Scavenging crabs and prawns will find it irresistible.

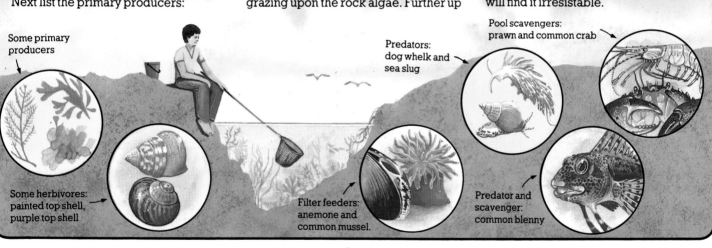

Some primary producers

Some herbivores: painted top shell, purple top shell

Filter feeders: anemone and common mussel.

Predators: dog whelk and sea slug

Predator and scavenger: common blenny

Pool scavengers: prawn and common crab

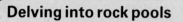

Oystercatchers probe the sand for shellfish

Look for terns diving into the water for fish and sand eels

Sanderlings run beside the water's edge after worms and crustaceans

What to do with oil-polluted birds

If you should find more than ten recently killed birds covered in oil in one kilometre of beach, contact the coast-guard immediately with full details. Birds stranded with oil-clogged feathers are difficult to save so contact a local conservation group for expert help. Keep the bird warm in a box and try feeding it with fish after a couple of hours. After two days clean the feathers using green washing-up detergent and a strong warm-water spray. Don't release the bird until its plumage regains its natural oils and structure as these provide buoyancy when it is in the water.

The wild side of the city

The city is a giant ecosystem in which man is the dominant species. It is the world's newest "landscape" and the only one created entirely by man. Urban ecology is always changing in response to man's technology, and our attitude to wildlife is changing too as pollution levels drop and some of our wild creatures venture back into the concrete jungle. The urban naturalist has much to discover right on his own doorstep, so use the projects suggested on these pages as a starting point in your exploration of the natural history of the city.

In the USA, raccoons love digging into refuse bins and in Britain, foxes have learnt the same opportunist habits.

How do animals see the urban jungle?

Get to know your city by taking a bird's eye view with the aid of a map. Plot all the parks, ponds, canals, rivers, sewage farms and gravel pits you can find for these are "islands" in the concrete that offer food energy and shelter for many species. From these refuges mammals and birds of prey may make nightly sorties into the streets whilst others creep in from the suburbs to pick at the food energy in what we throw away.

Try looking in these four habitats:

1. **City centres.** Look for descendants of cliff-dwelling rock doves now using the ledges of tall buildings for their roosting and nesting sites. Starlings have also learnt to do this. Watch for them flying in at night. Where have they been feeding during the day?

In Europe, residents encourage storks to nest on chimney stacks.

2. **In the park.** You can often see more animals here than in the countryside because they are so tame. Look out for exotic birds on ornamental ponds. Originally captive, many of these now breed wild and provide fascinating opportunities for observing courtship, feeding and nesting behaviour.

3. **Rubbish tips.** The waste we discard contains vast amounts of food that can be used by invertebrates, and the heat generated by decaying refuse enables warm-climate plants to thrive wherever their seeds are thrown out with the waste. Many birds (and bats too at night) come to tips to feed on the abundant insects there, and gulls regularly fly in to scavenge.

4. **Rivers, canals and reservoirs.** All inland waterways are worth exploring. Stroll along the banks looking for waterplants and birds. Where it is safe, look at the river strand line as you would a beach (p. 18). Remember to look out for interesting creatures in the mud.

How do plants get a grip on bricks?

Walls and paths seem poor places for plants, yet they survive even there – providing primary production which other creatures can use.

Look at a wall with no plants on it. Can you see a powdery green algae? That's *Pleurococcus,* and the first stage in the plant take-over. Next look for lichens. They root in the humus provided by dead algae and they help to break down the stone surface, so enabling mosses to take hold. Now look for weeds like ragwort and shepherd's purse, forcing their roots into the walls to form the higher level of this urban *plant succession.*

Lichens and mosses

Who likes waste ground?

If left alone for long enough, a whole community of plants and animals will develop on derelict land by a process of plant and animal succession, each stage preparing the way for the next. Many of the plants are regarded as weeds in gardens, despite the fact that they provide food for insects and other animals while many of our pretty garden plants do not. Find a piece of derelict land and try making your own ecological survey using these suggestions.

A line transect

Producers. See what plants are present. Recording the whole site would take far too long so take a sample using a "line transect". Stretch a string between stakes planted at either end of the plot and then record all the plants beneath the string. Note their names, the height they reach, and any insects that are on them. Identify the plants – they are the food resource for the other residents. Keep a record of the plants colonizing a newly cleared site.

Herbivores. Lay potato and other vegetable traps (see right) to sample the variety and number of herbivores. Use a pooter (p. 8) to collect small animals from plants, and don't forget to look under leaves and dead vegetation for insect larvae, caterpillars and grubs.

Carnivores. Place pitfall traps with bait (p. 8), and identify what you catch.

Larger animals. Are there runways, footprints, droppings, nests or other signs? (See p. 15). Mice and rats may be providing a source of food for local cats or even breeding owls or kestrels.

Making a street survey

Has your street got more wildlife than the next one? Try to work out just what yours has to offer by making a survey of each side of the street. Work your way along, noting signs of life on each house. Look closely and note the plants growing on walls, guttering, window ledges and on the bark of trees. Look amongst foliage for animal life, and put out traps and sticky jam-jars half full of water to sample the insect life. Enter your findings in a note-book like the one shown below.

What birds can you see (or hear) in your street? What time of day are they active? You might invent symbols for different species and plot them on a street chart each month throughout the year.

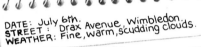

DATE: July 6th.
STREET: Drax Avenue, Wimbledon.
WEATHER: Fine, warm, scudding clouds.

No.	Notes
7.	House. Buddleia bush in bloom. Red Admiral butterflies. Sparrow in nest in roof gutter. Moss on window.
8.	Shop. Starling singing on chimney pot. Privet hedge and caterpillar. Spider in wall.
9.	House. Nettles and a flower? growing at base of house. Window boxes with pansies. Dandelions.
	Old Garage. ROAD. Bricks. Mouse run under. Rosebay Willowherb. Woodlice under bricks.

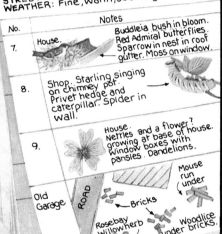

Potato trap

Side cut away to show animals inside. Make entrance level with surface. Hollowed-out potato.

Vegetable trap

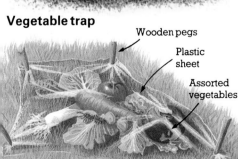

Wooden pegs. Plastic sheet. Assorted vegetables.

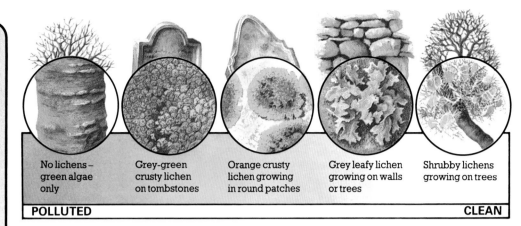

No lichens – green algae only | Grey-green crusty lichen on tombstones | Orange crusty lichen growing in round patches | Grey leafy lichen growing on walls or trees | Shrubby lichens growing on trees

POLLUTED   **CLEAN**

How polluted is your town's air?

1. Use the lichen scale above to estimate pollution levels in your area. The leafy and shrubby lichens on the right of the scale are very sensitive to sulphur dioxide (from car exhaust and smoke) which dissolves in rain making it too acid for them. If these lichens are present on stonework or trees, the air is usually clean but if only crusty lichens, as on the left, are found, the air is probably polluted. The most polluted areas have only green algae. Compare the lichens on tombstones and walls in different parts of your town.

2. The air is full of tiny floating particles. You can prove this by wiping the surface of an evergreen leaf with a white tissue and seeing what comes off. Measure your local particle pollution like this: take some stiff white card, say 20cm square, and cover it with clear plastic kitchen film. Coat the film with a thin layer of vaseline and put the card outside on a dry day. How long does it take for the test-card to get dirty? Look at the dirt under a microscope. It might contain pollen grains from a park or even soil blown from another country.

How to create a "pocket park"

There are many ways in which a city can be made a better place for wildlife – such as planting native trees rather than foreign species, and by making an effort to convert derelict sites and waste ground into mini nature reserves. This is quite a big job and needs a team effort, but it is an ideal project for a scout, guide or youth group. The aim is to create a natural environment including small areas of marsh, a pond, some trees and areas of rough grassland in which wildlife can thrive right in the heart of the city. It is an entire ecosystem in miniature. Surprisingly, neglected ground may contain rare or interesting species which can be encouraged in the park. Often, the hardest part is finding a site and getting permission to develop it. Find out if there is a project near you by asking at your library, community centre or conservation group. You could become part of the team. If there are no projects in hand, think about starting your own. You can check for vacant sites at your local planning office. Alternatively, search your neighbourhood for suitable sites, then prepare a report for your local environmental group who may adopt a site.

Inviting animals to visit you

There are lots of things you can do to encourage animal life into your garden, and most involve providing food, safe shelter, and nesting sites. If you have a garden it may be full of very pretty flowers but try asking yourself if it is really any use to wildlife. Many of the things we plant are useless to our native birds and insects. Before planting a new border, take steps to find out which flowers, shrubs and trees are most attractive to wildlife as well as to you.

Choose thick climbing vines to provide nesting sites; berry-producing shrubs for food; and flowers rich in nectar to attract insects. And don't forget the wild flowers on which many insects are totally dependent in their larval stages.

Today, wild habitats are disappearing all over the world, but if everyone tried to improve the facilities in their garden, wildlife would receive a valuable boost.

Wilderness corner

Elder bush

Sunflowers

Honeysuckle

In America, chipmunks may burrow beneath stone heaps

Wood pile

In Britain and Europe, a saucer of dog or cat food and some water may encourage a hedgehog.

Wild flowers

Wild creatures do not enjoy perfectly cut lawns and tidy flower beds! Wild, unkempt gardens are much richer in food for caterpillars and safe nest sites for birds. Try making part of your garden into a wilderness and you will be surprised at the number of species that will flock to it. The key is to provide a variety of food and shelter. Let the grass grow and encourage weeds like dandelions, nettles, thistles, buttercups and wild grasses. Privet, hawthorn, elder and holly are good shrubs for birds, and a screen of honeysuckle or ivy growing over a wooden trellis will provide perfect nesting sites. Piles of dead leaves, compost heaps, and bits of rotten wood provide a home for insects – and an additional food source for birds.

Encourage butterflies by planting nectar-producing flowers. Polyanthus and cat-mint are early flowerers and can be followed by aubretia, buddleia, hyssop and honesty. Try wallflowers and sweet rocket, michaelmas daisies and ice-plant, for later in the year. Keep a record of animals you attract.

Feeding birds

If your garden is full of insects and berries, many birds will be attracted. But you can supplement this with regular feeding too. In winter, birds may come to rely on the food you put out so don't start feeding unless you can continue without a break throughout the winter.

See what aids your pet shop has on offer. Peanuts in plastic net bags suit many small birds (though not in the breeding season) or you can make up, at home, a "bird pudding" by mixing bird seed and melted lard, letting it set in a yoghurt pot, and hanging this in a tree.

Some ideas for bird feeders

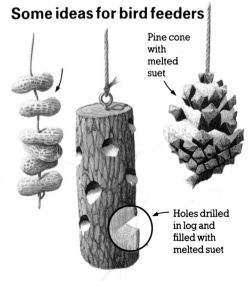

Pine cone with melted suet

Holes drilled in log and filled with melted suet

Bird feeders like those illustrated, plus half-coconuts and bits of bacon fat, can be suspended from a stick jammed across a window. The birds will soon get used to you watching from indoors.

A box for birds to nest in

Many birds are finding it harder each year to find suitable nest sites in the wild. You can help them by building a nest box and placing it in a safe part of your garden.

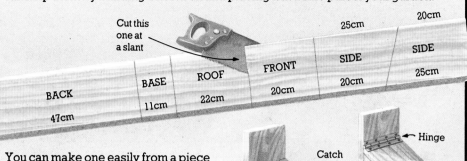

Cut this one at a slant

BACK 47cm
BASE 11cm
ROOF 22cm
FRONT 20cm
SIDE 20cm 25cm
SIDE 25cm 20cm

You can make one easily from a piece of shelf timber and some screws or nails as shown here. The size of the entrance hole determines which birds will use the box. A 29mm hole admits tits but keeps out sparrows in Europe, while the American house wren likes a hole 22mm in diameter, and the blue-bird one of 38mm.

Pine or deal is a good timber to use, treated with preservative once the box is assembled. Drill two small drainage holes in the bottom and hinge the lid to allow the box to be cleaned out during the autumn. At this time disinfect the box and give it another coat of preservative.

Siting is important. Face the box away from direct sun and the prevailing

Robin

Hinge
Catch
Nails
Entrance hole of correct size

weather. It can be fixed to a tree, a fence or even the side of the house, but should be out of reach of cats, say about 2m above ground. Put the box in place well before the breeding season so the birds can get used to it.

You could try building a box with a clear perspex back instead of a wooden back, and fix it over a hole in a shed wall so that you can watch from inside the darkened shed.

◀Some birds, such as the European robin, prefer an open-fronted box like that shown here. Site it as for the other box but amongst cover such as ivy or another wall-creeper. Don't disturb the nesting birds, as they may abandon the young.

Building a bird table

The simplest kind is a cake tin lid nailed to the end of a broomstick. A wooden tray on a stake also works well or you can build a more attractive table like that shown here. A roof will give shelter to birds and keep food dry but is not essential.

Siting the table is all-important. It must be safe from cats and not too far out in the open as some birds are uneasy when away from cover. Another method is to hang the table from a tree instead of placing it on a post. Place your table near a window so that you can record the species that come to feed – and note what food they prefer.

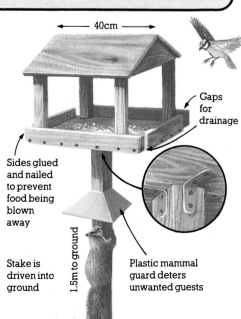

40cm

Gaps for drainage

Sides glued and nailed to prevent food being blown away

Stake is driven into ground

1.5m to ground

Plastic mammal guard deters unwanted guests

Helping bats to help themselves

Having your own colony of bats to study is something quite special – and well worth the effort. Make a box in the same way as for birds but don't treat the wood with preservative and don't drill an entrance hole. Instead, make the base piece 2cm shorter to leave a gap between the base and the back-panel. Roughen the inside with saw or nail scratches to provide a grip for the bats. Fix a number of boxes to trees or buildings, especially near a conifer forest (but do ask permission first). They should be placed where they can be warmed by the sun but not get too hot. Many of the bats are much smaller animals than one might think, and you may get up to 50 of the tree-nesting species crammed into a single box. But don't expect miracles. It may take anything from weeks to several years for the bats to accept the boxes. If they do, tell your local wildlife group.

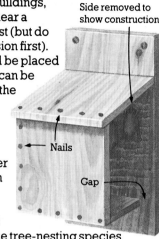

Side removed to show construction
Nails
Gap

Attracting wildlife with water

A pond, no matter how small, attracts a host of wildlife, and any of these ideas may work well in your garden.

1. **A birdbath:** any shallow container will do but a refuse bin lid placed upside down on bricks works perfectly.

Bin lid
Bricks

2. **Pond with plastic liner:** many books on garden planning will tell you how to excavate a pond and stock it with a variety of water-plants. You may even attract frogs or toads as well as birds.

3. **A tub pond:** a wooden tub or stone trough or sink can be sunk into the earth and stocked with water-plants. Small fish, snails and other pond creatures will thrive in it.

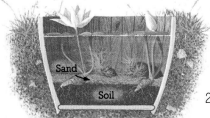

Sand
Soil

Making and using collections

Nature diary

Collecting is a good way of keeping a record of things you have seen, but the keen naturalist will want to go further and learn about the structure and classification of the animals and plants in his or her collection. This can help you understand more about the area in which the specimens were found. Museums have large reference collections which have been examined and catalogued by taxonomists (scientists who specialize in classifying living things). You can use these collections to help identify your own specimens, and also to look at specimens from other parts of the world.

In the past, many naturalists collected far too many specimens – sometimes filling literally hundreds of cases with eggs or butterflies. Even today, some so-called "nature lovers" destroy seashore life in their search for shells, or uproot wild plants, leaving no flowers to seed the ground. Make sure you are never one of these! Leave living things where they are: collect the evidence they leave behind – it is just as useful.

Specimen boxes

Card index

Hand lens (×10)

Tweezers

Mounted needle

Notebook

Tie-on labels

Collecting facts

If you are a good naturalist you will want to keep notes and records of your findings. They will enable you to compare past and present events, and improve your powers of observation. You could pass on your data to a society that may need it, or use your notes to help in your own conservation campaign (p. 31). Look at p. 32 for some useful addresses.

Field notes. Record the date and the weather, including wind, temperature and cloud cover as these affect insect and bird activity. Record the area and the exact location of your observations, and note the time of day they were made. Make quick notes and sketches of habitat, plants and animals; those you can't name can be looked up later.

Nature diary. This is your permanent record so it is worth taking care over presentation. Write up your field notes in a large hardbacked notebook or loose-leaf file when you get home. You can intersperse field notes with information from books and other sources, but make sure they are clearly separated. You can add sketches and photographs and even stick in small specimens here and there. You may like to keep a card index as well – say, by species. Index the diary once a volume is complete. It is not a difficult job and it makes the book so much easier to use at a later date when you want to look up just where you found a particular flower. See p. 30 for computerizing your information.

Labelling collections. Use tie-on card labels for large specimens and adhesive labels on boxes for small specimens. Write on the common name and Latin name of the specimen, and note the date and exact location of the collection site. Add a cross-reference to your notebook.

Collecting shells

On the beach or in your garden there will always be shells to find. Sea shells are common along the strand line (p. 18), along sandy beaches, and among rocks. Look for land-snail shells under bushes, leaves, stones and plant-pots. Bring the shells home and clean them carefully with an old toothbrush under a running tap. Visit your local museum or use a field guide to identify your specimens.

Small shells can be kept in glass or plastic tubes along with their labels. Matchboxes lined with cotton wool are good containers, especially if you cut a "window" out of the top and cover it with clear plastic. You may be able to buy a small cabinet with lots of clear plastic drawers (hardware stores sell them for storing screws and washers), or make a similar cabinet by stacking matchboxes.

Skulls, skeletons and antlers

You may be lucky and come across the skull of a sheep or goat, or something more unusual. Provided it is bleached white and clean, bring it home for your collection. Autumn and spring are good times to look for antlers (which season depends on the deer species). Skulls and other bones may be obtained from birds or mammals killed by the road-side or trapped in discarded bottles, or even brought in by a pet cat. Mounting a skeleton is difficult so concentrate on skulls alone at first.

The majority of the skulls you may find will need cleaning with only warm soapy water, but if the bone is still partly flesh-covered leave it near an ant nest or trail and they will do the job for you. Fix the skull with wire to a rock or tree so that scavengers can't remove it. A fresh skull should be placed in cold water, slowly brought to the boil, and simmered for two hours. The flesh can then be picked off with a needle and a pair of tweezers. Don't forget to clean the inside of the skull just as carefully as the outside. Once the flesh is removed, bleach the skull in hydrogen peroxide (obtained from a chemist) – but don't leave it in too long or all the teeth will fall out!

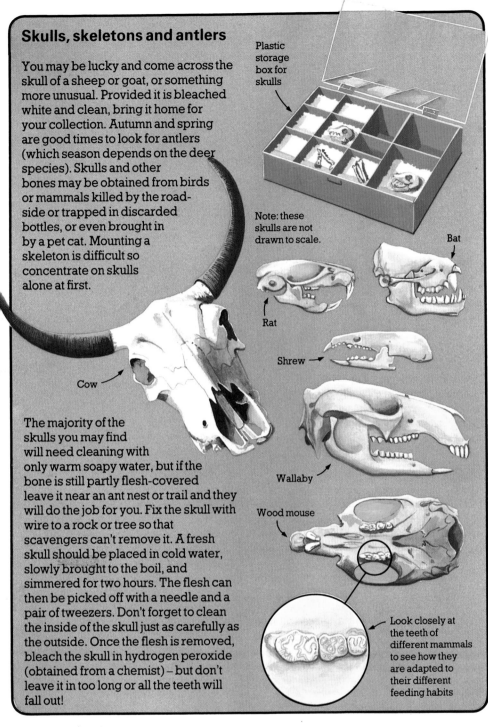

Plastic storage box for skulls

Note: these skulls are not drawn to scale.

Bat

Rat

Shrew

Wallaby

Wood mouse

Cow

Look closely at the teeth of different mammals to see how they are adapted to their different feeding habits

Finding out what the owls are eating

Many birds cough up indigestible bits of their food in the form of compact pellets. In the case of an owl the pellet consists mainly of fur and pieces of bone packed into an oval bundle between 2.5 and 7 centimetres long depending on the species. Search for them beneath known owl roosts.

Check barns, church towers, and old buildings for barn owl roosts

Soak the pellet in warm water for a few hours until the individual bits can be separated in a saucer by gently teasing them apart with tweezers and mounted needle. Sort the fragments into groups and then mount them on a display card as shown below. If you can identify the prey species from the skulls you will have discovered the owl's diet – *and* useful evidence about the local mammal population.

Look for pellets around owl roosts in hollow trees

Tawny Owl Pellet : August 15th. Hollow Oak Tree, Monk's Meadow						
LIMBS	SKULLS	JAWS	SKULL FRAGMENTS	VERTEBRAE	RIBS	FUR

More on collections

Fungi, mosses and lichens

These can be collected easily in the field but some are getting scarce, so take only a few specimens. Fungi will rot if put in a plastic bag so use an open container like a basket lined with paper. Wooded areas are the best places to look, but beware: many fungi are poisonous. *Don't eat them,* and wash carefully after handling them.

Use a knife to scrape small samples of moss or lichen from trees or rocks. Dry them at home on a radiator and store them in envelopes or small boxes labelled with the species' name.

Many of the woody bracket fungi can be dried to give very attractive exhibits for a home natural history collection. Look for them on tree trunks and stumps.

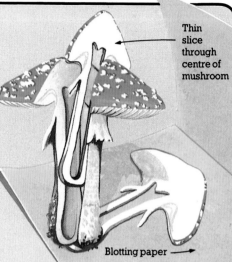

Thin slice through centre of mushroom

Blotting paper

Mushrooms are difficult to preserve but if you take a very thin slice right through the middle of the cap and stem, and then press it between sheets of blotting paper weighted with a pile of books, you can take a very good imprint. Colours fade very quickly so make notes, sketches or photographs before you pick fungi.

Preserving spiders' webs

Find a good web and spray it carefully with aerosol paint. White looks best. Paint or spray a thin layer of glue onto a sheet of matt black card and bring it up close to the web. Press it into the web, avoiding any sideways movement that may tear the web. Cut the supporting threads (the spider will soon make another) and finish off with a protective layer of spray varnish.

Plaster cast collections

You can make casts of animal tracks, tree bark, fruits and many other things using quick-drying plaster of Paris. You will need a plastic container (a large yoghurt pot will do), some 30cm × 5cm strips of card, vaseline, an old spoon, paper clips, a large container of water, and a trowel.

Animal tracks. Vaseline the inside surface of a card strip and form it into a ring, securing it with a paper clip. Press the ring into the soil to make a containing wall around the footprint. Mix up sufficient plaster in your pot by adding plaster powder slowly to the water. The plaster mix should have a smooth creamy consistency. Pour the mix into the retaining ring until the print is covered by at least 2cm of plaster. Leave for about 20 minutes then use the trowel to dig beneath the cast so that you can lift it up along with the underlying soil. Let it set overnight, then brush off the loose earth.

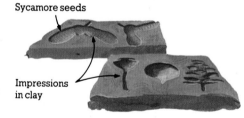

Sycamore seeds

Impressions in clay

Fruits and seeds. Find some tree seeds like chestnut, sycamore or hazel and make an impression of them in a block of modelling clay. Build a low wall of clay around the edge of the block and pour in the smooth plaster mixture. Let it set in the mould then peel away the clay. You can paint the seeds and mount the block for display.

Tree bark. Choose a tree with deeply furrowed bark then take a 10cm square of modelling clay and hammer it over the bark with your fist. Peel it away carefully and proceed as described above. A collection of bark casts, all painted in their natural colours, can be mounted on a board and then hung on the wall.

Carding a snake skin

Snakes regularly shed their skins as they grow. If you find a skin, cut it along the side of the belly and open it out. Make sure it is the right way out (the skin is rolled inside out as it is shed) and mount it on card.

Card

Paper clip

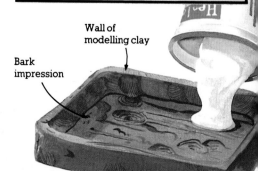

Wall of modelling clay

Bark impression

Recording wildlife sounds

What tape recorder is best?

Apart from being great fun, making sound recordings of wildlife can often reveal completely new data. Very few bird species, for example, have had all the variations of their songs and calls recorded.

An ordinary cassette radio-recorder works well, and the small "personal" models are very convenient. When choosing one, make sure the model records clearly, has a counter, and has easily accessible controls. Use the long-life, high-power type of battery and always choose good quality tapes with a high frequency range.

When you are looking for a recorder, look for one with a manual recording level control. Automatic levels cannot cope with the short sharp sounds that animals make and the result is a rather poor recording. Unfortunately not many models have manual control and those that do tend not to be cheap.

Using the equipment

Get to know the animal you wish to tape by first observing its habits. Having chosen the best place from which to make your recording, get into position with your equipment – making as little noise as possible. By stalking you can often get quite close, but don't forget the potential of a hide (pp. 12/13). Keep the machine in the recording mode and use the pause button to start and stop while you monitor the sound through a pair of headphones or an earphone. At the start of each recording, speak into the mike softly to record the date, the location, weather and additional data. Make separate notes in your notebook and don't forget to include the numbers showing on the recorder counter dial.

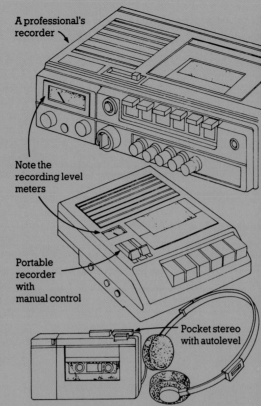

A professional's recorder →

Note the recording level meters

Portable recorder with manual control

Pocket stereo with autolevel

Choosing a microphone

Most recorders have an integral microphone which is adequate for general use but a separate mike is more versatile. The mike may pick up finger movements if hand-held so tape it to a stick. An extension lead will allow you to place the mike near a nest while you record from a safe distance.

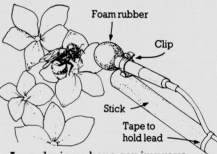

Foam rubber

Clip

Stick

Tape to hold lead

A good microphone can improve the quality of your recordings a lot. They vary in shape, size, cost and directional sensitivity. The best for general use is a cardioid mike, also called a uni-directional mike. It tends to dampen out sounds not coming from the direction in which it is pointed, so it is good for birds.

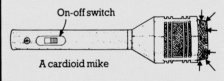

On-off switch

A cardioid mike

Even better, but much more costly, are the rifle mikes (or gun mikes) used by professionals. They are very sensitive, but only in a narrow forward beam, and will pick out an individual bird in a distant tree.

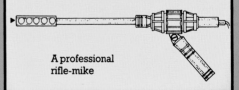

A professional rifle-mike

Ideas for recording projects

1. Garden birds at the bird table.
2. Animals at the zoo.
3. Frogs croaking at night.
4. Your local dawn chorus of birds.
5. Bees at work among flowers.
6. Your pet dog, cat or bird.
7. Play back your recordings to the bird or animal that made them. What happens?

BOFFIN'S BOX

Making a parabolic reflector

You can greatly improve the directional quality of a cardioid mike by placing it in a curved dish to concentrate the sound. A professional will use an expensive parabolic reflector but you can make your own by poking the mike through the bulb hole in an old car headlamp reflector. Point it in the direction of the sound you wish to record.

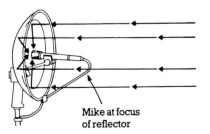

Mike at focus of reflector

Even better – try an umbrella! It acts like a huge sound-gathering dish and if correctly focussed it should enable you to record a bird at the far side of a large field.

Fix the mike to the stem of the umbrella, facing *into* the dish and about 15cm from the apex. Monitor the incoming sound and move the mike to find the best position along the stem. The sound-gathering performance of your umbrella/reflector can be greatly improved by spraying the inside with a thin layer of a metallic silver paint.

Mike

Microphone lead

Nature through the camera's eye

This page provides some tips on how a camera can help the naturalist. You can photograph nature with any camera but the more you know about technique, the better your photographs. Reading books on photography will be a great help, but learn how to use a simple camera well before buying an expensive one. And wherever you are, always remember the wildlife photographer's code: "The welfare of the subject is more important than the photograph."

Using a simple camera

No special equipment is needed to record a view, or the habitat in which you found a particular specimen. A simple camera using 110, 126 or 35mm film will record the colour of a fungus before it was picked, or the changing face of the landscape through the year. Remember to make notes when you take photographs.

Camera types

126: Easy cartridge loading. Simple operation; limited use.

110: Cartridge loading but the small 16mm film size produces poor enlargements.

35mm: The best. Film in longer lengths and cassette loaded. More complex to use.

A panorama can be built up from a series of overlapping photographs like this. To make sure the pictures are at the same level it is best to use a tripod.

Visual records

Why not take pictures of collections you no longer wish to keep? Group the specimens on a large sheet of plain paper and place a clear label next to each one. Slide film is best for this.

Taking pictures of wildlife

Most wild animals are shy and difficult to approach, so taking pictures with a simple camera may not be easy. Some of the "pocket" cameras have an in-built telephoto lens that magnifies the image. These are a great help but to get good photographs you must either get really close to the animal or use a powerful telephoto on a more advanced camera.

Deer taken from a car window with 50mm lens.

The same deer but with a 200mm lens.

The SLR camera

A single lens reflex (SLR) camera enables you to use a whole range of lenses and other accessories with just one camera body. This means you can adapt the camera to a wide range of situations, which is ideal for nature photography. As animals are forever on the move, often from a well-lit area into shade, automatic exposure setting is very useful, but you may want a camera with manual override as well.

Such cameras are expensive but second-hand bargains can be found.

A 200mm or 300mm telephoto will cost quite a lot but is ideal for nature photography. You should use this type of lens with the camera on a tripod to avoid camera shake. Tele-converters can double or treble the power of smaller lenses but unless of top quality they give poor results. Wide-angle lenses give a wide field of view and are good for working in confined spaces or to photograph landscapes.

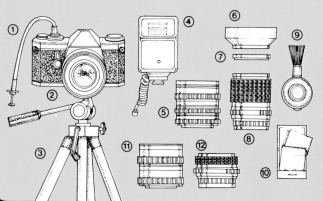

Equipment to aim for

1. Cable release.
2. SLR camera and 50mm lens.
3. Tripod.
4. Computer flash and long lead.
5. Extension tube set.
6. Lens hood.
7. "Skylight" filter.
8. 135mm telephoto lens.
9. Puffer lens brush.
10. Lens tissues.
11. 2 × teleconverter.
12. Wide-angle lens.

Ways of getting in close

1. Use a hide (see p. 13). (Even with a hide you'll probably still need to use a telephoto lens). Try using the hide near a bird feeder. Take pictures through the car windows when in a safari park.
2. Visit the zoo early in the morning when there are few visitors, but *never* poke your lens into a cage or pen except under the supervision of a zookeeper.

Choosing film

Use black and white film when you are experimenting – it is much cheaper than colour. And when you get it developed, ask for a *contact sheet* first. This is one large print containing all your pictures at a small size. You can then choose which to have printed larger.

Colour prints are ideal for illustrating your nature diary or building up your reference collection. Colour slides (transparencies) are cheaper per shot and can be viewed on a screen. Their detail is good and you can get colour *and* black and white prints from them.

The ASA rating of a film measures the speed with which it reacts to light. In bright light use slow films (25-100 ASA) as these produce better quality prints when enlarged. Faster film (200-400 ASA) gives a "grainy" print but is needed in poor light and in close-up work.

Nature in close-up – photographing small things

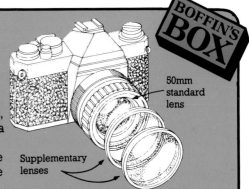

BOFFIN'S BOX

The world of close-up photography opens up a vast new range of things for the naturalist to capture on film. The miniature world of insects and flowers is suddenly available – and without the need for a lot of expensive equipment.

Some 110 cameras have special lenses built into them so that you can photograph small objects in close-up. If you have a 35mm camera you can use a supplementary lens, or a combination of them, screwed onto the front of the standard lens so that they act as a magnifying glass. They are quite cheap and come in varying strengths. Alternatively, there are a number of systems, designed for SLR-type cameras, all of which work on the principle of moving the lens further from the body of the camera in order to increase the image size on the film. Which you choose depends on the amount of magnification you want – and how much you can afford!

50mm standard lens

Supplementary lenses

1. Extension tubes

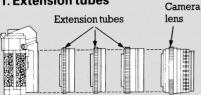

Extension tubes

Camera lens

These are by far the cheapest way of getting high magnification for insect shots or flower details. The tubes, or rings, can usually be bought either singly or in sets of three. Placed in various combinations between the camera lens and body, they produce varying degrees of magnification to suit the size of the subject being photographed. Focusing is critical so choose non-moving subjects and use a tripod whenever possible.

Try using extension tubes with a telephoto lens. This will enable you to photograph easily-disturbed insects from much further away while still filling the frame with the main subject.

Move in slowly to the subject you wish to photograph and support the telephoto on your knees

2. Macro lenses

These are designed for close-up work and are ideal for small subjects such as insects. Instead of magnifying the image from a distance, macro lenses let you focus on the subject at short range. This means that your subject will fill the frame. The macro facility is available on many lenses, including telephotos, and all can be used with extension tubes or bellows for greater magnification.

50mm macro lens

3. Bellows units and telescopic tubes

Here the lens is placed at the end of an extending bellows tube which produces infinitely variable levels of magnification instead of increasing it in stages as happens when you use extension tubes. However, the unit is bulky and some manufacturers now make a telescopic tube which combines the lightweight advantages of extension rings with the higher magnification of a bellows. These systems produce the magnifying power needed by professionals.

Extendable telescopic tube

Bellows unit

Setting up the subject

Let's take a caterpillar on a leaf as an example. In the field you may need to brace the plant by tying it to a stick to stop it moving in the breeze. Make sure the caterpillar is well lit and place the camera in position, preferably on a tripod. The smaller the aperture you use, the greater your depth of focus will be – so use the smallest aperture that conditions will allow.

Alternatively you could bring the caterpillar home on a piece of its plant and stand it in a pot with plain paper or card behind it (see below). Set up the camera and focus very carefully on the caterpillar, then take the shot with a flash gun held to one side on an extension lead.

50mm standard lens only

50mm lens plus supplementary lens

Fully extended 50mm macro lens

50mm standard lens with extension tubes

50mm standard lens with bellows unit

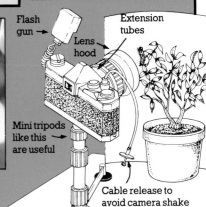

Flash gun

Extension tubes

Lens hood

Mini tripods like this are useful

Cable release to avoid camera shake

Looking ahead

New technology in nature

A microcomputer can cost you less than a good camera, yet it will help you store the information you collect, it will analyze that information ("data"), compare one site with another, or examine records from different times of the year – all far faster than you could ever manage by looking through notes in a book or filing system.

All you need is the "micro" itself, your television to act as the display unit, a cassette for storing programs and data, and a tape recorder. (A program is a list of instructions telling the computer what to do.) Card index or record file programs can be bought on cassette and loaded into the micro using the tape recorder. If you are a skilled micro-user you may wish to write your own programs. Some of the smaller micros may require an additional memory pack, called a RAM pack, to store all the data.

T.V.

Micro computer

Keyboard for typing in instructions

Tape recorder

Extra memory packs like this 16K RAM pack plug into the back of the micro shown.

As an example, let's see how a micro could help you with your birdwatching. Assuming you have the correct program, each day you could feed in information about the birds you have seen (see p. 12). You would have to decide on just what information you wished to record, but it might include the time of day, the date, the weather conditions, what the bird was doing, what tree it was in, and so on.

Once you have a good data base of several months' or years' records and the appropriate program, you can begin asking the computer questions such as, "On which days did I see swallows?" or "What species have I seen in oak trees?" or "Which birds most commonly sing on cloudy days?" The micro can even be programmed to draw you a graph showing how the bird population changes through the year, or a pie-chart of the relative abundance of the various bird groups in different habitats. The possibilities are endless.

Computer cards and phone-ins

Information is a powerful tool in aiding conservation. Send the data you collect to an organization that can make good use of it. Natural history societies often have special cards which you can fill out with details of plants, mammals, insects and birds that you have seen. These records are then put on computer and can be used for drawing up the species distribution maps.

Another way of gathering information from amateur naturalists is by asking people to telephone their sightings to a special number previously given in newspapers, magazines or on local radio. Help is always needed to cope with the response. A bird migrant phone-in is a regular annual event for the members of the Young Ornithologists' Club in the U.K. If you want to join this club, or a similar one, see page 31.

Tracking animals

Technology enables scientists to follow animals far beyond visual range. Here are four examples of new methods now in use.

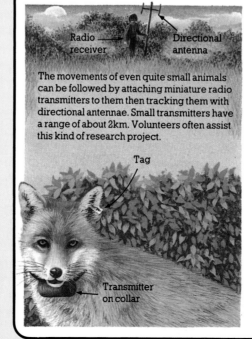

Radio receiver

Directional antenna

The movements of even quite small animals can be followed by attaching miniature radio transmitters to them then tracking them with directional antennae. Small transmitters have a range of about 2km. Volunteers often assist this kind of research project.

Tag

Transmitter on collar

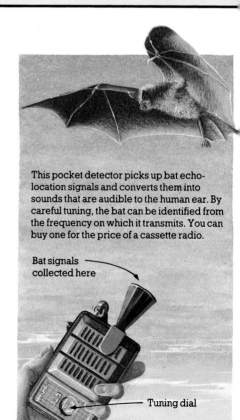

This pocket detector picks up bat echo-location signals and converts them into sounds that are audible to the human ear. By careful tuning, the bat can be identified from the frequency on which it transmits. You can buy one for the price of a cassette radio.

Bat signals collected here

Tuning dial

How to contact your local wildlife group

If you need some help in starting your own project, or would like to help with someone else's in order to learn more, then joining a local conservation group is well worthwhile. These groups have experienced naturalists who will be glad to help. They often run outings to areas of special interest, and most groups organize projects like marking nature trails, making animal and habitat surveys, and running renovation schemes.

There are several different kinds of group, organized locally, regionally, nationally and internationally. Not all of them have junior membership schemes so make sure you choose one that does. A selection of the main groups is given on page 32. Your local library will probably have the names and addresses of the people to contact. Active groups always need more members. Check wildlife magazines for details of, say, a "Young Ornithologists" club or a "Conservation Volunteers" group. Local radio stations may also help you in your search and many actually have schemes of their own. You really can learn a lot more by being part of a club than simply by reading lots of books – and club activities are also great fun.

Standing up for nature

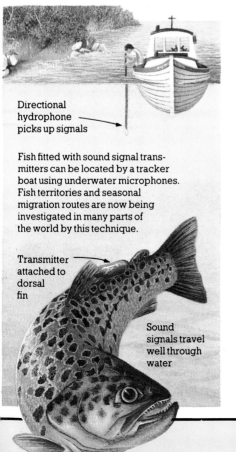

All over the world, nature is being crowded out by man. Valuable wildlife habitats are being destroyed by river pollution, and by industrial projects, and even new parks are often designed with very little regard for natural history, when simple improvements could make them so much more valuable for man and animals alike.

You as an individual *can* do something about it – *if* you make your views known. Perhaps you know of a derelict area that could be made into a Pocket Park (p. 21), or you hear of group of trees about to be felled, a pond due to be filled in, or an oil spill on a beach. If you feel strongly about it, write to your local paper or wildlife magazine. Letters to council planning departments from young naturalists often make people sit up and take notice: it may well be something they didn't even know about. To protect wildlife, you have to stand up for it.

You could start up your own newsletter with a group of friends, writing about the natural history of your local area. Ask people to send in stories, put them down on paper, perhaps with some sketches and photographs, and get someone to make copies – at school or in an office. People will soon be asking for the next edition! Try sending some of the articles to wildlife magazines: they may use them.

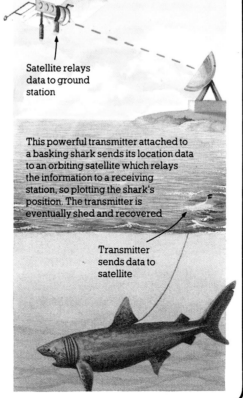

Directional hydrophone picks up signals

Fish fitted with sound signal transmitters can be located by a tracker boat using underwater microphones. Fish territories and seasonal migration routes are now being investigated in many parts of the world by this technique.

Transmitter attached to dorsal fin

Sound signals travel well through water

Satellite relays data to ground station

This powerful transmitter attached to a basking shark sends its location data to an orbiting satellite which relays the information to a receiving station, so plotting the shark's position. The transmitter is eventually shed and recovered

Transmitter sends data to satellite

Careers in nature

You may be thinking of working for nature in the future. Here are some suggestions to consider. Contact a careers adviser for further help.

Zookeeper. Try for a summer job as an assistant to learn what it's all about.

Park Warden/Ranger. This entails looking after nature reserves. Experience as a volunteer will count in your favour.

Landscape gardener. An outdoors job, planning parkland and private gardens.

Agriculture. Plenty of scope for a keen naturalist. Try summer work first.

Teaching. There is a need for biology teachers at Field Studies Centres and Adventure Centres as well as in schools.

Museum work. Classifying species and putting exhibits on display for the public.

Environmental control. Monitoring pollution. A job requiring good qualifications.

Research. Work as a laboratory technician or scientist. You may need a degree.

Biologist. Lots of important work to be done in fisheries, forestry and farming.

Publishing. Producing books like this one, as a writer, designer or illustrator.

Radio and television. Gathering information and putting together nature programmes.

Societies. Information groups, conservation groups and others, all need organizers.

Veterinary science. Medical care for household, zoo and farm animals.

Wildlife photographer. Photographing nature for books and magazines.

Books and addresses

Spotter's Guides for Europe (Usborne)
Spotter's Guides for U.S.A. (Mayflower)
Totem Guides for Canada (Totem)
Collins Field Guides for Europe
Peterson Field Guides for N. America
Rigby Field Guides for Australia
Book of Nature Photography by Heather
Angel (Michael Joseph)
Butterfly Culture by J.L.S. Stone and
H.J. Midwinter (Blandford Press)
Mammal Watching by Michael Clark
(Severn House)
Gardening with Wildlife (National
Wildlife Federation)
The Seashore Naturalist's Handbook by
Leslie Jackman (Hamlyn)
Using Urban Wasteland by
S. Loggenburg (Bedford Square Press)

British Trust for Conservation Volunteers, 36 St Mary's Street, Wallingford, Oxfordshire OX1 0EU, U.K.
Council for Environmental Conservation, Zoological Gardens, Regents Park, London NW1 4RY, U.K.
WATCH, c/o Royal Society for Nature Conservation, 22 The Green, Nettleham, Lincoln LN2 2NR, U.K.
Young Ornithologists' Club, The Lodge, Sandy, Bedfordshire SG19 2DL, U.K.

National Audubon Society, 950 Third Avenue, New York NY 10022, U.S.A.
National Wildlife Federation, 1412 16 Street NW, Washington DC 20036, U.S.A.
Sierra Club, 530 Bush Street, San Francisco, Ca. 94108, U.S.A.
Canadian Nature Federation, Suite 203, 75 Albert Street, Ottawa KIP 6G1, Canada

Association of South East Field Naturalists' Societies, P.O. Box 1369, Mount Gambia, South Australia 5290
Victorian Field Naturalists' Clubs Association, c/o Natural Herbarium, South Yarra, Victoria 3141, Australia
Gould League, c/o Public School, Mary Street, Beecroft, New South Wales, 2119

Index